First published in the UK in 2018 by Illusion2Reality
Publishing
graham.moneyroots@gmail.com
Copyright © 2018 Graham Bridger

ISBN: 9781983061899

Scripture quotations taken from the Holy Bible,
King James 1611 Version

Converging Signs and Rejection of Truth

Thanks

I want to start by giving thanks. First, to my wife who has taken the brunt of spending so much time alone whilst I have been tucked away in my study writing this book. Second, to my good friends, David Paul and Steve Dodgson, for taking the time to provide help and advice in its preparation. Third, to all those fellow believers for helping me over these past few years to think about what the Bible teaches about the last days (Eschatology). And last, but certainly not least, to the God of the Universe through whom Jesus Christ came to this earth just over 2,000 years ago to show us what truth really is.

The initial inspiration to write this book came from dreams the Lord gave my wife about the Second Coming of Jesus over thirty years ago at the beginning of our Christian lives. We have held these and other precious revelations from God in our hearts ever since. However, the impetus to put pen to paper was birthed when the global debt crisis hit the world in 2008. This near catastrophic event set me on a course of research that would reveal political, economic, financial, technological, cultural, ecological and spiritual events happening throughout the world, all converging together and pointing to teaching in the Bible about 'the last days' and the 'Day of the Lord'

Table of Contents

Foreword

As the title of this book indicates, we are living during unique times, with the world experiencing what are so often described as 'unprecedented' events that are causing huge levels of uncertainty and confusion amongst millions of people all over the world. I wonder how many people notice how this word 'unprecedented' is used by the media more than any other to describe what is happening. As soon as we turn on the television to watch the news or open our daily newspaper, the word unprecedented seems to be used to describe political turmoil, economic problems, financial indebtedness, revolutionary technological development, social and cultural change and ecological disruption. In fact, such is the magnitude of what is taking place across the globe, even stronger words are often used to describe what is happening. Words like Armageddon, catastrophic, and quite often, Biblical. With so many 'unprecedented' events occurring at the same time, is it any wonder that so many people feel insecure and fearful. What I find particularly interesting, is how the media so often choose the word Biblical. I think the assumption is that that it connects to 'end of the world' scenarios and is therefore likely to attract more readers. The question is, is there any truth in this applied assumption? Why are these events happening now and more to the point, is there any particular significance as to why they should be happening at the same time? After all, throughout history, unprecedented events including volcanic eruptions, earthquakes, fires famines, floods and of course, wars have always taken place, the severity of some, often resulting in the loss of millions of lives. It should be no surprise that people living at the time thought that they were facing the end of the world. But we must still ask, do these signs mean the end of the world?

Many people will say that most strange phenomena taking place can be answered by scientific analysis but research demonstrates that this is not always the case. Conclusions can often be regarded as inconclusive, some purely speculative and others merely conspiracy theory. What is the average person to make of all this? Most people probably conclude that as no-one really knows, it is probably better to put the matter out of their minds and just get on with living each day at a time.

Over the past ten years, I have been studying much of the material made available in the media and other sources alongside the Bible to try and gain a more biblical perspective about what is happening, particularly from a cultural context. As a Christian, I believe that the Bible brings much understanding and great insight into why these events are happening and why now. Provided we look at the broader picture that the Bible provides, we can begin to 'see the wood for the trees'. In other words, provided we don't allow ourselves to get bogged down with the detail of each event, we can begin to 'join the dots' to see the bigger picture. When we do, I believe that we will understand that not only are these events linked, they are converging and leading towards what the Bible teaches will take place as we move into what it describes as the end of the end days.

I am very aware that over the years, numerous individuals have made many attempts to set dates for the end of the world. It seems that mankind has this inert desire to deal in conspiracies and the intrigue of end of the world scenarios as can be seen by the attendance of thousands at Hollywood movies that capitalise on this phenomenon. What is clear however, is that each so-called prediction about the second coming of Christ or the end of the world that hits the press has always proven to be false. Every time, this happens, the Christian faith is ridiculed and the name of Christ treated with disrespect and mocked.

What most people do not realise is, that the Bible teaches quite clearly, we are not to try to determine dates for the return Jesus or to predict dates for the end of the world, for it tells us that no-one but God the Father knows. However, what is not generally understood, is that Jesus did expect his followers to know the season of his second coming just as he did for his first coming, which was also clearly prophesied in the scriptures. No matter what we may think about' end of the world' stories, we can't base our understanding on Hollywood movies and the like.

If people realised how accurate Bible prophesies have been proven over the years, they might stop to consider why the relatively small number remaining that speak about what will happen at the end of the world should not be equally accurate. But despite the number of Christians who are faithfully upholding Biblical truth and attempting to bring warnings about what it has to say about the times in which we are living, so many are regarded as fear mongering and even as slightly unhinged. Thus, the warnings are disregarded by most and this includes a significant number of church leaders who have failed to teach the whole of scripture that should include Eschatology (the study of the end times) for nearly half a century.

As we consider what is happening in this hectic, entertainment based, hedonistic, complex world full of propaganda and fake news, I believe that there is one vitally important question to be asked. Is there such a thing as absolute truth? If there is no such thing, then it seems that anything goes. Everything becomes relative and meaningless. There is no real reason or purpose for being alive. But if absolute truth does exist, then this changes everything. For it means that every human being can find out why they exist and what their purposes are whilst here on earth. It means that they can find out what happens after their death.

In this book, I want to present first, a brief understanding about what is happening in the world and to then consider what the Bible has to say about the events or signs that are taking place to reveal the direction in which mankind is travelling in the days that lie ahead. In order to set the scene for the rest of this book, I will briefly touch on some of the things that are happening.

I would suggest that the two foremost examples are, firstly, when the world experienced what became known as the 2008 'Global Debt Crises' we all experienced the near collapse of what had become a fatally crippled banking system. The world was submerged in financial debt. To try to deal with the consequences triggered by this calamitous event, governments have been imposing severe austerity measures ever since. Their economic policies are resulting in reduced levels of incomes and falling standards of living across the Western world. This in turn is causing substantially reduced demand for goods and services and a decline in economic growth which is exposing serious deficits in investment, major funding programmes and pensions bringing anxiety to millions of people whose future expectations are very unlikely to be met. The Bible makes it very clear that the money system will play an important part in the rise of the final authoritarian government during last days.

Converging Signs and Rejection of Truth

The second example is perhaps the most amazing to have occurred in the last 70 years. It concerns the restoration of a tiny country that was destroyed and the population scattered to the four corners of the globe over 1,800 years ago. This was when Israel was reborn and became a nation again in May 1948. Such a thing has never happened in the history of the world, but in the book of Isaiah in the Bible this was prophesied. For a country to be reformed and its people return from countries all around the globe after all those years; then to see its original culture and Hebrew language restored is truly a miracle. Since then, another miraculous event prophesied in the Bible has also come true; the recognition of Jerusalem as Israel's capital by the US Trump administration.

To take another example, millions of people are flooding into Europe as they flee from the ravages of wars and the abuse of power in Middle Eastern countries. As a result, migration continues to rise to levels never seen before which is creating political and social division. At the same time, there has also been an increase in violent crime and terrorism, often perpetrated by Islamists. It is leading to the infiltration of other religions, particularly Islam, into Western countries and will again play an important role in the demise of the truth of the Christian faith.

In the Bible, in the book of Matthew Chapter 24, Jesus tells us that as we approach the time of his second coming to the earth, we are going to witness disturbing events throughout the world rising in number and intensity. It teaches that these events will cause levels of stress never seen before and never to be seen again. It states that they are caused by nothing other than the implementation of a clear satanic agenda and an ideology which is making a last concerted effort to reject the truth of the Gospel of Jesus Christ in order to make way for the coming authoritarian reign of the person the Bible calls the Anti-Christ (which means 'in place of Christ'). The Bible clearly teaches that as the world moves into these last days, the spirit of the Anti-Christ will have increased in its power over the world causing ever greater traumatic events to occur, the intensity of which will eventually cause the final falling away, or apostasy by many from the Christian faith. It tells us that at the pinnacle of this world-wide disruption, the Anti-Christ will manifest in physical form to commence his authoritarian rule over the earth, declaring himself to be, and accepted by nearly all people groups throughout the world as god.

Many Bible scholars and Bible teachers believe, and I agree, that we are now witnessing the last stages of the distortion and rejection of the truth that Jesus declared that is resulting in nothing less than the collapse of all moral framework of our Western society. This is being caused by the infiltration of ideology that is designed to become the orthodoxy of our age. One such individual has referred to it as a form of cultural colonisation and, another, the establishment of man-made ideologies which usually lead to totalitarianism. It is similar to, but different from, communism or fascism but it still holds as its goal the creation of a utopian society where everyone is equal. It involves a reconstruction of reason and understanding and a denunciation of anyone who holds to a belief in the God of the Bible. It needs to be understood that this is presaging the last stages of what the Bible describes in the book of Ephesians as a spiritual battle against the spiritual forces of evil in the heavenly realms. It is a war to end all wars and it is to the death, physically and spiritually. But why is it happening?

An Age-Old Battle

The Bible provides us with the answers. It is nothing less than the age-old battle between good and evil, fought ever since the creation of the world. The battle between the 'spirit of the prince of the power of the air (Satan), working in the sons of disobedience' and the spirit of Jesus Christ who came just over 2,000 years ago to reveal who God is. He was God incarnate and he came face to face with evil. He is described in the Bible as the suffering servant who showed mankind a depth of sacrificial love never seen before. He showed us what love is and despite being faced with the intensity of this evil, he was prepared to suffer the most horrendous death on the cross so that mankind may be set free from this evil.

This anti-Christ 'spirit' has, in these last days, been causing social and moral change that is staggeringly swift and historically unprecedented. All this is bringing fear to many people. There is turmoil and disruption everywhere. People are struggling to make sense of it all. Against this background, stress levels, particularly amongst younger people, have been rising with reports now showing substantial increases in mental illness. What is particularly perturbing to many, is the sheer speed of change taking place in these days; it seems to be increasing at an exponential rate. It is interesting to note that despite most people remaining unaware of the significance of this ideology which confuses the meaning of truth, there are still many people, both Christian and Non-Christian, who are speaking out vociferously and articulately in support the basis of the Judeo-Christian foundations for life which claims absolute truth. Melanie Phillips, a Times columnist, and Professor Jordan Peterson, a clinical psychologist at Toronto University, are two prominent people speaking out about these new ideologies, recognising how so few people seem to be able to see through the subterfuge of what has become an 'all about me' 'godless', materialistic, consumer driven, entertainment orientated Western world. The former chaplain to the Queen, Dr Rev Gavin Ashenden has spoken out in the same way, recognising that the pan-sexual revolution taking place throughout all Western societies is taking us all along the road towards authoritarian rule. However, the people exposing this ideology say it is a very lonely battle to get people to 'think' and appraise their western lifestyle and consider where they need to apply their time and energies so as to prepare themselves for what we will all be facing in the near future.

I am reminded of the famous book *'War of the Worlds'* by the author and futurist H. G. Wells. It is all about human life on the earth being systematically obliterated by an invading Martian army who arrived from the 'red planet' in their giant three-legged machines to create devastation all around them. Fortunately, the aim to destroy all human life was thwarted when the attackers finally succumbed to the most well-known virus known to man: the common cold. But this is pure fiction. Today, we find ourselves in the last stages of another kind of 'world war' but this is not fiction. No, it is not another Martian invasion or even a military war that could involve the use of nuclear weapons, although only God knows how close this could still be, judging by the way world leaders act towards one another. I suggest this war is, in fact, far worse, because, in its sinister way, it seeks to systematically obliterate all conscience and reason in the lead-up towards the establishment of a utopian view of the world which will turn out to be just the same as every other previous authoritarian rule. But this utopian world, whilst seemingly similar in its longer term aims, is the same as the H.G. Wells depiction - nothing less than the complete subjugation of mankind. It is the final manifestation of the Anti-Christ 'spirit' that operates with specific purpose in each age.

How does such an Anti-Christ spirit operate? One way this can be illustrated is to look at the laws of the land. These were once founded on the Bible and rooted in the Judeo-Christian faiths, but it now appears that governments throughout the West are increasingly passing laws that, in effect, especially view Christians as 'bigots' and potential enemies of the human race. An example of how this has come about is through the passage of 'equality' and 'hate' laws. Increasingly, it seems that many Christians are now being compelled by these laws to compromise the very religious beliefs that inspire their lives The former leader of the Liberal Democratic Party in the UK, Tim Farron for example resigned in June 2017 when he was asked several times by a very zealous interviewer whether he believed, as a Christian, that the act of homosexual sex was a sin and replied "to understand Christianity is to understand that we are all sinners". He was subsequently hounded by the press for several weeks until he stated that he could no longer hold the position as party leader. In a resignation speech he had not expected to give, Farron was defiant that he could not compromise his faith, even for the party he loved. "I joined our party when I was 16, it is in my blood, I love our history, our people, I thoroughly love my party," he said.

"Imagine how proud I am to lead this party. And then imagine what would lead me to voluntarily relinquish that honour. In the words of Isaac Watts, it would have to be something 'so amazing, so divine, it demands my heart, my life, my all'."

It is also worth noting that the media, business and entertainment industries are actively promoting this anti-Christian sentiment in the minds and hearts of individuals, families and institutions every single day. In fact, references to people being bigots or racists is becoming increasingly common in the media, where presenters often interview Christians very aggressively, with a preconceived and dogmatic point of view.

It appears that there is a hostility to Christianity arising which is not just occurring in one or two parts of the world but across the whole of Western society. We have now reached a stage where the post-modern culture no longer believes there are such things as absolutes. It is now promoting the notion of total equality which finds no place for the absolute declaration of the Bible that says Jesus is the only way to God. I believe that whilst Christians throughout the ages have held on to this fundamental belief through all kinds of persecution, that often resulted in death, the real question, when push comes to shove is whether Christians today will do the same in the face of ever increasing persecution that is surely coming.

With the Bible proclaiming that it the source of all truth, it is likely that those Christians who adhere to its teachings, particularly regarding issues about sexuality, will find themselves and the Bible itself brought into question as being suitable to teach modern day society. I believe we have reached a point where every professing Christian will have to choose between two options: to cave in to the 'spirit of the age' or risk persecution just as thousands of Christians throughout the persecuted world do every day.

It ought to cause us to ask the obvious question: how should Christians respond to such rapid cultural change that is increasingly anti-Christian? Further, how should church congregations be prepared for the days that lie ahead? It is disappointing that few Christian leaders seem to grasp the significance of the changes and identify the Biblical signs now taking place. It is clear there is a lack of church leadership and direction. As it says in the book of Proverbs 29:18

'Where there is no vision, the people perish'

Without Christian leaders having a clear understanding of what the prophetic scriptures have to say about the times we are in, any sense of hope will be based on wrong expectations moving ahead. Further if people reject the God of the Bible as the source of all hope, people will find themselves drawn into the last days deception that Jesus spoke clearly about. Whether we realise it or not, if there is no God of creation who knows everything from the beginning to the end and each of us intimately, then there can be no hope. The last book in the Bible is 'Revelation'; it is the revelation of Jesus Christ and his last words to the world. In this book, Jesus warned the church what to expect in the future for all those who love God and for all who choose to finally reject Him. Revelation means unveiling. We are watching prophetic events being unveiled in our time. It is as if the curtain is going up to reveal what is happening, but it is only for those with eyes to see and ears to hear.

Anyone who studies the Bible will realise that what is going on is not some sort of conspiracy theory; it is the outworking of Biblical Prophecies. Moreover, the Bible says these things *are* going to happen. Many people do not realise that to date, every single prophecy in the Bible, has, over a few thousand years been fulfilled with complete accuracy; for example, the creation of the state of Israel in 1948 after the Jews were exiled from their Promised Land some 2,500 years ago. Many Bible teachers believe that only a few prophecies are left to be fulfilled and these speak mostly about the future for mankind. If we are to think about what the future might hold, it would be wise to consider the sheer weight of evidence based on the unequivocal accuracy of these ancient writings. It has been accurate about the outcome of history to date, so why should it not be about the future.

In this book, I will examine how the spiritual forces of evil are manifesting themselves, primarily promoting the belief that all religions and ideologies of 'worldly' love are somehow leading us in the direction of one God for all. This pathway is, in fact, leading to the obliteration of truth, mass deception and a great apostasy; put another way, it is the rejection of the true faith, as Satan prepares what the Bible declares as the harlot Church whilst Jesus prepares the true church. Once again, the

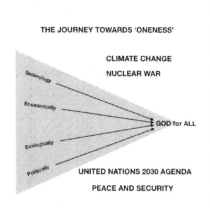

THE JOURNEY TOWARDS 'ONENESS'

CLIMATE CHANGE
NUCLEAR WAR
Technology
Economically
GOD for ALL
Ecologically
Politically
UNITED NATIONS 2030 AGENDA
PEACE AND SECURITY

human race seems to have arrived at the same place where it started.

In the account of Babel in Genesis, the first book of the Bible, man sought to rule the world; man is still trying to rule the world by building a Utopian society. Of course, there is no such thing as utopia and never will be in this life on earth because of the sinfulness of man. However, this does not stop the arrogance of man believing otherwise. In order to achieve this end, it is necessary to build this new ideology which promotes equality through the concept of what is being called 'Oneness' or 'brotherhood of man' and it is in a very advanced state of implementation across the world. It requires that the Biblical values previously known and understood be opposed and replaced before the last great authoritarian ruler comes into power prior to Jesus Second Coming.

I believe we are now living during the final lead up to the greatest event the world will ever see: The Second Coming of Jesus Christ. A shaking of all the foundations of our previously accepted world 'systems' is now taking place and it has become clear that things are changing in the spiritual and natural realms. The sheer scale of confusion and turmoil that Jesus described in the Bible, will require a faithful church to be able to take a stand against the onslaught of this evil until he comes the second time. For many this will be very hard as the Bible prophecies that Christians will be marginalised which will make sharing the gospel of Jesus Christ subject to serious persecution. As we consider these things in the light of Biblical scriptures my reasons for writing this book are fourfold. First, to consider the evidence and meaning of the various 'Signs'; the events now happening throughout the world and the church and their connection to the end time Biblical scriptures. Second, to urge church leaders to consider how the provision of eschatological teaching from the prophetic scriptures can best prepare people for the days that lie ahead. Third, to encourage people to discover how, through the use of personal testimony, the God of the Bible can break into people's lives and change them forever; and lastly, to provide a permanent record for the benefit of my family and friends of how God changed my life and also that of my wife's. I want to know when my wife and I are with the Lord that my children and grandchildren who we love dearly will remember the vital importance of knowing Jesus in this life and the next.

It has not been my intention in writing this book to provide detail into each 'sign' or event but an overview that will hopefully provide an understanding of the 'big picture' to enable people to 'join the dots'. My hope is that readers will be persuaded to carry out their own research in order to gain insight themselves about what is happening in the world and in the church today and do so by setting aside time and energy to study the scriptures for themselves. What is important is that we extract what the scriptures actually say, the discipline known as *exegesis,* and not as so many others do, read into the scriptures our own beliefs of what is true through the practice of *eisegesis*. There is a desperate need for the Holy Spirit to enlighten us of the truth of these scriptures during the difficult days that lie ahead. I pray that God will bless you in your studies.

Chapter 1: 'It Speaks of the End'

There will be those reading this book who may well be asking themselves is there really a God at all? Before moving on to examine in more detail what is happening in the world and in the church in the days in which we are now living, I want to share with readers some of my background about how my wife and I became followers of Jesus Christ.

After leaving school I spent just over 13 years in retail banking. The rest of my career was spent in the Financial Services Industry as an Independent Financial Adviser. During my career the world experienced a significant global stock market crash which had a profound effect on me and all those who I was serving. This occurred just four months before my wife and I became Christians. I had responsibility for managing several millions of client's savings and pensions at the time and I was deeply affected by the aftermath of this crisis.

Converging Signs and Rejection of Truth

The stock market crash happened at the time we witnessed a great hurricane on the 16th of October 1987. It occurred just after midnight, following an infamous weather forecast by Michael Fish on television that evening that it was not going to happen. But it did happen and it literally wiped out millions of trees and damaged much property and landscape in the south of England. We stood at our bedroom window pressing the glass to prevent it from buckling during the early hours and saw some fairly large trees in our own garden blown away with the intensity of the wind. Then, the following Monday morning, I drove to work and saw debris scattered everywhere and trees blocking many roads. All was eerily quiet. After arriving at my work place, my normal routine comprised of hanging up my coat, switching the kettle on for the usual morning cup of coffee and walking past a bank of computers and switching them on one by one as I walked to my office before checking the post. I would then walk back down the corridor and glance at each computer to see what the markets were doing across the world. As they powered up, I was stopped in my tracks as I noticed the first screen showing the Far East market had turned completely red, meaning that a huge downturn had occurred. As each screen powered up the same thing happened: all the world markets were showing massive losses. It was such a surprise that I found myself tapping the front of the screens with my knuckle, just as if they were a barometer and by doing so, you could somehow change the direction of the weather being forecasted.

Converging Signs and Rejection of Truth

The morning of 17th of October, I was watching the worlds stocks markets collapsing together in front of my eyes. I then realised all my clients' funds were being devastated. This event became known as the 1987 World Stock Market collapse. Looking back, I believe that these two events, occurring simultaneously, were major signs of things happening in the both the natural and the spiritual. In both those events, I was helpless; I could do nothing to stop the trees being ripped up and nothing to stop my clients' hard-earned savings and investments disintegrating before my eyes. I couldn't even telephone any brokers to sell any stocks, because the telephone lines became clogged and in any event the London Stock Market was forced to close. This was followed in the next few days by a deluge of clients desperate to know what had just happened and what I was going to do to save their investments. It was the beginning of the downfall of my company, but it was also the point at which God was about to step into both mine and my wife's lives. Our decision to give our lives to Christ came only five months later in February 1988 and shortly afterwards God led me to leave the company. Throughout the following years, I continued in business, creating other financial services enterprises until September 2008, when I had expected to retire. However, at that moment the world suffered from what became known as the Global Debt Crisis. This turned out to be far worse than the stock market crash that occurred at the beginning of my business life 30 years previously.

This book is a culmination of a thirty-year journey for my wife and I since we both became Christians. We are both still amazed at the way God brought us to the saving knowledge of Christ on the same day in February 1988 whilst in different parts of the world. It was through reading two books by the same author. I was reading *'Is Anyone There'* on a flight to the USA to search for a new business model following the crisis; my wife was reading *'Live a New Life'* whilst at home as she contemplated what the future might hold. The author David Watson, was a very well-known leader in the Church of England and respected evangelist. Both my wife and I responded quite separately to the call to accept Jesus as our Saviour which completely changed the direction of our lives. Because neither of us had any religious or church affiliation, the gospel message struck both of us like a 'bolt from the blue'. Having been brought up in atheist families, the concept of God was never part of our thinking or conversation during the previous twenty years of marriage. My attendance at a Church of England School and my wife at a Convent, served us little in understanding God, other than to put us off any form of 'religion'. After leaving school, we had no connection with 'church', other than to attend the usual quota of weddings, christenings and funerals that most people seemed to do in those days whether they believed in God or not.

The Dream – Second Coming of Christ

Shortly after our conversion to Christ, God gave my wife an astounding dream about Jesus coming again and her meeting him in the heavens together with millions of others. She woke me in the early hours of the morning out of a deep sleep to tell me. Neither of us could understand the reasons for receiving it, or what it meant, because we  had never read or, for that matter owned a Bible. Shortly thereafter, a mature Christian at the church we were then attending was able to point to all the different scriptures that were in the Bible that confirmed the exact details of the dream. Both my wife and I have held this dream close to our hearts over all the years since then, somehow believing that it did speak about the times we are now experiencing. Something had been birthed inside us which carried a sense of urgency about the need to see people come to the knowledge of God that propelled me into evangelism.

Over the next couple of months after this first dream, God began to give my wife other dreams, as well as Bible verses that I believed were particularly relevant to me. The scriptures were always relevant to whatever I was thinking at the time or answers to questions that I had been asking God in my own mind. Although we found this baffling, we also knew they were from God; although she had no idea of what was going through my mind, these scriptures chimed with what I was thinking at any particular moment in time and therefore resonated in our hearts. Whilst they did not always seem to provide me with the answers I might have been looking for, they nevertheless encouraged me to press on. However, the scripture that gripped me most occurred at the beginning of our Christian lives from the book of Habakkuk.

"Then the Lord replied:
"Write down the revelation and make it plain on tablets
so that a herald may run with it.
3 For the revelation awaits an appointed time; it speaks of
the end
and will not prove false, though it linger, wait for it;
it will certainly come and will not delay

The impact of it has remained as strong today as it was then. It astounded me because it was clear that the Lord had heard my question and answered it. We had no idea what it meant at the time but felt in our spirits that it had something to do with 'the end'. The reason was simple: it was because it resonated so strongly with the dreams.

The dream of Jesus Second Coming began to totally change my Christian perspective. Initially, the impact caused me to become involved with evangelism for most of our service in the church. However, during the first couple of years after our conversion, I attended a nine-month course in London with John Stott at the Institute of Contemporary Christianity. It was here that I began to wrestle with what they called 'Issues Facing Christians today'. At the end of the course, all the students had to write a thesis on what they believed God was saying to them. Mine was about the need to build the church and I entitled it '*I believe in the Church*', because I had been so impressed by the book of the same name written by David Watson. It was in this thesis that I first began to question church life and style and it was where I first wrote about my early impressions of church. It was because of David Watson's appraisal of the world and his understanding and description of sin and salvation that we chose to give our lives to Christ. Following this, my attendance at John Stott's course made me aware of Jesus intentions for his church. Having been a non-believer for so many years, I still considered attendance in traditional church boring and irrelevant. This was of course because I obviously had no idea or experience of what was meant by Christian community or fellowship. I went on to read all David Watson's books and began to gain a personal understanding of his desire to see church built around New Testament principles. The example of his life became the major influence on me for the journey that was to come.

Chapter 2: Converging Signs – What is Happening in the World?

As stated in my opening chapter, I believe that during the past ten years, world events have been occurring to produce greater political turmoil, vast amounts of unrepayable financial indebtedness, revolutionary technological development, social and cultural change and ecological disruption. It is clear that they are not only unprecedented, but they are converging and causing huge levels of uncertainty and confusion. In this chapter I provide an overview but in the following chapters I look at each area in a little more depth.

Whilst there has always been political and economic disruption throughout the world, the rapidity of the changes has been all the more difficult for people in the Western world to grasp, because for the most part, the majority have lived a relatively comfortable lifestyle since the end of the Second World War. In truth, many of us have been wrapped up with a consumer driven, materialistic understanding of life but for perhaps the first time in history, events are shaping up that are affecting the whole of the Western world at the same time and threatening our perceived way of life. However, they are leading to further events clearly prophesied in the Bible.

The World Economic Forum, has become one of the most prominent annual events to gauge what is happening globally. In 2018, it was attended by about three thousand CEOs and Managing Directors from the largest Multi-National Corporations, as well as Presidents and Prime Ministers and numerous other leaders from all over the world, including royalty. These business and government leaders and other attendees are some of the most influential people attempting to grasp the sheer complexity and magnitude of the challenges they face.

The Forum debates are extremely interesting, because the public get the opportunity to listen to so many top experts as they try to grapple with the ramifications of economic, political, environmental and technological change and why they perceive the need for a common approach to solutions. It is just one of a number of major 'Think Tanks' that discuss issues facing mankind, but it is possibly the most influential. Others include the Council of Foreign Relations in the US, Chatham House in the UK and the more controversial Bilderberg Group to name but a few. Apart from the Bilderberg group, where agendas are generally kept secret and the public and media excluded from the gatherings, they all seem to attract the world's most influential people.

What is clear, is that despite the wide-ranging discussions that take place with many different viewpoints, the seriousness of world events still tends to favour globalism as the only means by which world problems can be solved. This ties in with the wider utopian view now being promoted world-wide by the United Nations Agenda 2030 where the aim is to reaffirm that peace and security can only be secured and the continuation of the planet assured through combined action. The Agenda's aims are to solve the world's biggest problems, like global warming, poverty, the supply of clean water and the need for education for all, to name a few, all by the year 2030. However, I believe that such agendas are really nothing more than an unattainable utopian vision for the future. More on this later in a later chapter.

Globalism

The title of the 2018 Forum was 'Creating a Shared Future in a Fractured World'. The discussions revolved around the far-reaching ramifications facing mankind due to the speed of advancing technology during what is being referred to as the 4th Industrial Revolution. It was acknowledged that the world has been experiencing a series of unprecedented, cumulative events and is now in unchartered territory, with no-one really knowing where it all might lead. Once again, it was agreed that every corporation and government in the world must now work together in order to be able to deal with the ramifications.

Converging Signs and Rejection of Truth

A 'Globalist' view was therefore imperative because of the staggering sheer speed of the changes which are proving hard to get to grips with. This should tell us that we are in for change beyond anything experienced to date and we all know that people do not really like constant change.

This year, many of these leaders agreed that there had clearly been a kind of mutiny amongst the people in many countries throughout the western world. It was acknowledged that millions were very unhappy with the implications of the 4th Industrial Age that is coming upon us. Interestingly, this unease has manifested itself in many other ways and for different reasons as well, but none so apparent as the recent decisions taken by the British electorate to reject membership of the European Union and by the American public to embrace Donald Trump as their President. The chair of one of the groups felt that this demonstrated that there had been a clear cry of anger by people who felt they had been abandoned by their leaders. She went on to say that she believed that these were the moments when the forgotten spoke and people found their voices to reject the advice and guidance of so-called experts and the elite everywhere. I also believe that in the last few years before 'Trump' we also saw other rebellions taking place throughout Europe, as ordinary citizens saw the great heavy hand of the European Union descending upon any country falling out of line, where any form of real democracy was overturned by globalists who, many believe, really do rule the world.

Global Debt

But I believe that this rejection needs to be put alongside the financial crash, which brought home to people the fact that only a very few individuals working in the financial sector were able to accrue huge rewards with the rest of us then called to pick up the bill when their greed led the world astray. So, taken together, we are living in a world of widening, not diminishing, financial inequality, in which many people are seeing their standard of living faltering, but also their ability to earn a living at all disappearing. Clearly, there are many who now believe that the elite bankers effectively 'ripped off' the population during the 2008 Global Crisis, leaving everyone else to carry the full financial burden into the future.

People in Western nations are now wrestling with unprecedented change and they are finding the implications difficult to grasp. This is because the majority have lived through a lengthy period of exceptional and rapid economic growth since the end of the Second World War. What most do not realise, is that this growth has been based mainly on increasing levels of indebtedness which has produced a false sense of security. These feelings of relative comfort have also been created because of continually advancing technological progress, enabled by advanced computerisation and the availability of a cheap energy elixir (drug) called oil that finances and maintains the vast infrastructure. But in 2008, everything suddenly changed when a sense of reality was injected into this illusion of well-being. The continuing increase in world debt finally reached unsustainable levels and culminated with the near collapse of the entire world's monetary system. As a result, Central Banks throughout the world stepped in and began to print huge quantities of money, but instead of calling it money printing, they invented a new term that most people wouldn't really understand; they called it Quantitative Easing or QE for short. The injection of unprecedented amounts of new money into the system was meant to be a temporary stop gap measure, lasting probably no longer than six months during which time, it was hoped that the world's financial markets would stabilise once again. But the system had, in reality, suffered from a severe financial heart attack so to speak and needed emergency care. The care and medicine administered (QE) has now been going on for over a decade and the economy has not recovered. Nothing on this scale had ever been attempted before and no-one knew what the outcome of such vast amounts of money printing might do to the world's economies. The economy (patient), is still breathing because of the artificial stimulus it is receiving but if it were removed it is clear the patient would die.

Incredibly, the level of debt that caused the crisis in the first place has since doubled and now stands at over $250 Trillions which is quite impossible to repay. It equates with approximately four times the entire worlds gross domestic product (GDP). The only way any reductions could have been made were if world economic production had increased dramatically which has not happened. In fact, quite the opposite has occurred. Expectations for continuous growth are falling dramatically across the world. The consequences for having lived in this illusory world for the past seventy years are now coming home to roost and we are watching a debt time bomb ticking away that will lead to the disintegration of all paper wealth on the planet.

The reality is that there has been a wholesale abandonment of trust in the Western banking systems due to their investment of public deposits into high risk securities, rigging interest rates in their favour and other criminal acts including and involvement with money laundering and drug money. Fines have been imposed in the multi-trillions but not one senior banking official has ever been brought to account in any meaningful way. Instead the public have witnessed governments bailing them out with public money and paying out executives in the hundreds of millions by way of bonuses, golden good-byes and large pensions also in the millions. Have their actions really changed over the past ten years? The answer is no, because they still make profits in the hundreds of billions and their way of honouring all their deposit holders has been to reduce interest rates to virtually zero which has destroyed the income of millions of people. The question is – why don't banks care more about their customers? The answer is because, Central banks have been printing billions in new money and making it available to the banks at virtually no cost. The banks have little need for customers deposits and no reason to pay them any interest on their savings.

Converging Signs and Rejection of Truth

Clearly, the Global Debt Crisis still presents serious problems for our entire world's monetary system as will become more and more evident in the months and years ahead. The intensity of various issues facing mankind are causing governments throughout the world to believe they must act together.

Man's Destruction of the Planet

The threat of climate change has been with us for many years but the sense of urgency has dramatically increased in recent years with many eminent scientists proclaiming that mankind is literally destroying the planet. Stories of unprecedented ecological destruction are being reported daily, including a considerable increase in the number of earthquakes and volcanic eruptions, raging fires, devastating floods, severe famines and a variety of strange weather conditions. One day we hear of huge hail stones the size of tennis balls in mid-summer causing untold damage to property and cars, the next day droughts and reports of mass animal deaths across the entire globe, many of which scientists are unable to offer any scientific explanations. Interestingly, the late Professor Hawking, commented in the Guardian Newspaper last year saying *"Now, more than at any time in our history, our species needs to work together. We face awesome environmental challenges: climate change, food production, overpopulation, the decimation of other species, epidemic disease, acidification of the oceans. Together, they are a reminder that we are at the most dangerous moment in the development of humanity. We now have the technology to destroy the planet on which we live but have not yet developed the ability to escape it".* His comments were reinforced by other eminent scientists, some of whom have even suggested that we could actually be nearing the end of the world.

The sheer urgency of the situation has caused the United Nations to launch what they call their 2030 Agenda for Sustainable Development now adopted by nearly every country in the world and supported by all governments. I cover more on this in another chapter on the environment.

Cultural Change, Equality and 'Oneness'

Another strange phenomenon is occurring throughout Western society. For a variety of reasons, we are now seeing an all-embracing strange ideology emerging that is sweeping the Western world. Governments, institutions and major corporations are forming a common approach to and general acceptance of the idea of what I call 'Oneness'. The word 'Oneness' tries to capture and describe the thinking behind a world-wide adoption of an ideology of equality that many would simply refer to as either extreme socialism or Marxism. Some people have described it is as identity politics and others cultural Marxism. In adopting this ideology, it appears irrational argument without supporting facts is put forward based on subjective issues and feelings and a large number of people in Western societies have been lured into this self-seeking, 'me orientated' way of thinking but the question is, what is behind it?

Converging Signs and Rejection of Truth

A Change in Human Behaviour

It was the former Prime Minister Harold MacMillan who famously said 'We've never had it so good'. He was referring to the post war years following the end of the Second World War, during which time Western economies continued to grow each year. Unlike the previous generations faced with the realities of war, where children became adults very quickly, millions of people have, during the past 20 years or so, become totally consumed with an amusement orientated, consumer driven, materialistic and hedonistic lifestyle where highly advanced technology has become more and more captivating. Somehow, amusing and enjoying ourselves became a preoccupation. There are many reasons for this. Clearly, the degree of increasing pressure that people are exposed to in recent years in this 24/7, always available, high speed communication world is a main factor, but technology and particularly communication technology became intoxicating and a constant and serious intrusion into family life. Finding ways to amuse ourselves, not only became an industry in itself with promises of a utopian future, it became a way to seek relaxation away from the stresses and pressures of life. In addition, the now infamous social media platforms have created their own, rather unique pressures in that they have changed the way humans interact with one another. We now see adults, youth and even children walking in streets, towns or sitting together in restaurants, cinemas and parks with fingers rapidly pressing keys on their mobile devices and their heads glued to screens, devoid of all conversation. This phenomenon is unlikely to improve as technology continues to entice and where the internet is positioned to become even more intrusive in the future.

In whatever way we may regard this total change in human behaviour, numerous studies confirm the addictive nature of such technology. It is acknowledged by many professionals as having become a fundamental reason for depression, anxiety and even suicide especially amongst the youth of today.

Amusing Ourselves to Death

Aldous Huxley's famous novel *Brave New World* was written in 1931 and tells the story of a futuristic society with genetically modified social classes. People are trained to put society first, not the individual.

The climax of Brave New World occurs in the final chapter when Mustapha Mond's scientific or sociological experiment with John the Savage comes to an end which, in Mond's mind and in the minds of his citizens, confirms their **World** State way of life. That way of life is in the mantra: Community, Identity, Stability. An ideology was quietly being imposed where amusement was taking the place of thinking and reading. This theme was stated once again in book 'Amusing Ourselves to Death' written by educator Neil Postman in 1985. The book's origins lay in a talk Postman gave to the Frankfurt Book Fair in 1984. He was participating in a panel on George Orwell's *Nineteen Eighty-Four* and the contemporary world. In the introduction to his book, Postman said that the contemporary world was better reflected by Aldous Huxley's *Brave New World* whose public was oppressed by their addiction to amusement than by Orwell's work, where they were oppressed by state control. However, the sinister spirit behind this ideology now gripping the Western world is the same force that is attempting to imprison humanity once again but it is now reaching its final stages.

The Zeitgeist (The Spirit of the Age)

Most people have never heard the word **Zeitgeist.** In modern dictionaries this word is described as the Spirit of the Time or Spirit of the Age. The word **Zeitgeist** is originally an expression in German. The spirit (Geist) of the time (Zeit.) It announces the conceptual and cultural environment of a period of time. It is interesting that this 'spirit' or influence is acknowledged in the Bible as being the 'spirit of the air' that causes human beings to focus mainly on themselves and their own desires. It is not something people are consciously aware of, but the influence is always there, a voice somehow whispering in our ears about the need to satisfy our own lusts all the time. Once again, people tend to misinterpret the meanings of words. The word lust is all too often associated only with sexual overtones, but in fact it simply means 'I want it now'. We can't wait because our inner desires have been aroused and we must satisfy them now. So, what is the conceptual and cultural environment in which we find ourselves at this moment in time?

In reality, the cultural environment has been the same ever since the days of Adam and Eve. The Bible tells us about how they were told by God that they could have anything and go anywhere in the beautiful Garden of Eden, but they must not eat of the tree of knowledge, because if they did they would lose their innocence and know good from evil and surely die. As with anything humans are told NOT to do, they immediately want to do it. Just test yourself to see. If, as a young student of 20 you were led to the greatest library in the world and told that you could read any book you like, more than you could ever read in your whole lifetime, but that you must not read the book that says 'Not to be read under the age of 30'. What do you think you would want to read first? Why is that? We seem to be born with this inert desire to rebel against authority. The Bible describes this spirit as a spirit of rebellion where the influence comes from a being called Satan. The word means adversary. The Bible continues to use this same language and speaks of this spirit of evil overcoming human beings unless they choose to be set free by Christ. Humans have always shown that they are mainly concerned with themselves and we know from the seven deadly sins how humans seem to be affected by this spirit. Let's remind ourselves what these seven deadly sins are: Lust, Gluttony, Greed, Laziness, Anger, Envy and Pride. I am sure that there is not human being on earth that could say they have never suffered from one or more of these and sometimes many at the same time.

This 'Zeitgeist' is something happening to us. The Bible tells us clearly that it is a spirit of Satan that is driving a world view. It is a view that excludes the God of the Bible. It is the same spirit that denies the authority of Christ. The Zeitgeist of this age has opened the door to the ideology of equality, but this is a very clever ideology because it uses words whose meanings have somehow been distorted to mean something quite different. The theme is to create a new culture and draw everyone together in a spirit of 'Oneness'.

This is nothing less than the return of Marxism but somehow disguised. It also seeks to ensure that people adhere to the need for a one world view for solving the world's problems because of their perceived enormity. The question is - are we going to trust man's utopian vision of the future or are we going to trust the God of the Bible who has already given us a clear picture of what lies ahead? With this 'spirit of the air' driving an unconscious agenda it has become clearer how and why strange ideologies happen on a such a wide and diverse scale. Whatever utopian views of the future may be projected, the Bible clearly prophecies what lies ahead in the end times and tells us how people are going to react and how they need to prepare.

This Zeitgeist or spirit of the age has also been identified by writer for the Times, Melanie Philips. She speaks about it as the formation of a kind of 'Brotherhood of Man' attitude. It is, in fact, a level of deception that the Bible warns us will face humanity in the last days. It tells us that it will rise to levels never before experienced as it moves towards the eventual acceptance of the man the Bible calls 'The Lawless One'. It will require a Marxist belief in equality that other writers including Steve Maltz and Professor Jordan Peterson have described as 'Cultural Marxism' or 'Identity Politics'. It has created nothing less than a sexual revolution that challenges all the basic tenants of the Bible. It is in the process of neutralising sexuality by saying that feelings trump facts and denies all scientific and biological evidence of the difference between man and woman. Nothing could be more destructive to God's creation of family life. The Bible tells us in the book of Isaiah that a time will come when good will be regarded as evil and evil as good.

The politicising of the sexual revolution through equality laws combined with the requirement to act unilaterally in the struggle to find a common approach to the problems of climate change by all nations is being reinforced by United Nations 2030 Agenda for Sustainable Development, Peace and Security. It sets the exact scene required for the Biblical prophecies regarding the rise of the Anti-Christ. It is perhaps one of the most important events in determining where we are in the last days, because it concerns our understanding of morality. It is, in reality, the very same sign that has been attempting to deconstruct our understanding of sexuality for centuries but it has now rooted itself in the law of the land.

Converging Signs and Rejection of Truth

The Christian Persecution of the West

Because everyone in the West is now living in an entertainment-based, technologically addicted, rush and tumble world, anti-Christian laws are being passed right under our noses with very little resistance from many Christians or the church at large. As a result, it seems that not so subtle persecution is growing insidiously. Over the last few centuries, it has, in the main, been possible to declare the Christian gospel message freely to the benefit of society, however, increasingly, the signs are that these days are numbered. In many other countries, the consequences for speaking out the Gospel through evangelism are often severe and can even result in death. But the Bible tells us that authorities will come against all Christians everywhere who speak the truth as we move into the end times.

Curtailing the Right to Free Speech

So, how should Christians be thinking? I believe that they have some important choices to make. The Bible clearly tells us that we will have trouble in this world, although Jesus has overcome the world and he gives us the power to do the same. It seems that more and more, Christians are going to have to begin to reshape their desires and expectations in line with what it teaches. The reality is, that we now live in a society that is curtailing the right to free speech. Once this occurs, we are on the road towards authoritarianism. Throughout the West, many Christians with responsible jobs and careers are now being persecuted, often losing their positions, because they proclaim the good news of Jesus Christ. Those Christian leaders of the past, who were previously highly regarded for strong and ethical Christian values, are now being ridiculed as bigots and hate speakers. Christian organisations, for example, 'Christian Concern' are dealing with legal cases where Christians are being persecuted each day. In fact, Christian Concern itself is being labelled by some as an 'extremist' organisation.

Who Rules the World?

The Bible tells us clearly, that God's creation of the world was perfect. He provided laws that would enable mankind to live in perfect harmony with Himself. But, mankind rebelled against these laws in order to choose their own pathway. This has, over the centuries, seen the sins of man spreading throughout the world, with their actions no longer under the love and protection of their maker. No longer having a divine understanding, mankind had placed themselves under the spirit of Satan (a mighty fallen angel), who the Bible says, is the father of lies, deception and death. That is why, in the New Testament, we are told Satan controls the world. As a result, mankind continues to listen to the voice of the spirit of the Zeitgeist influenced by a satanic spirit as he seeks his own way and his own solutions. If mankind concludes that there is no

God, then we should not be surprised with any number of potentially disastrous outcomes. But the Bible tells us that God made the whole universe and only He has complete authority over everything. Satan's rule is temporary and limited and everything he does still comes under God's overall authority. But the good news is, that it is possible to remove ourselves from the power of this satanic rule, because God has made a way through the death and resurrection of Jesus Christ. We have been given the Holy Bible, which is God's word to mankind. In this book we are given understanding about how the world was created and how it is going to end. Perhaps more importantly, whereas science cannot answer many 'why' questions about the meaning of life, the Bible can and does.

Now, in the light of the wide-ranging number of seemingly impossible global problems, it is apparent that people will be persuaded towards global solutions, which will also provide the perfect opening for a global approach to government and Religion.

With the current levels of political turmoil, dissatisfaction and dissension taking place throughout the Western nations, it appears that democracy is under threat. Indeed, there are voices stating that that ordinary uninformed people should be prevented from voting on highly complicated issues about which they have little understanding. This belief has certainly been heard during the current Brexit struggle to free ourselves from the grips of the European super-state. Many believe that democracy has largely been 'managed' across the European Union countries since the 2008 global crisis, as ex bankers have been installed, through money and influence, into positions of power. The following article was written by Stephen Foley in the Independent Newspaper in November, just after the 2008 Global crisis began.

"If there's something weird in the financial world, who you gonna call? Goldman Sachs. The US government, involved in a firefight against the conflagration in the credit markets, is calling in another crisis-buster from the illustrious investment bank, this time Goldman's most senior banker to finance industry clients, Ken Wilson. And so, with this appointment, the Goldman Sachs diaspora grows a little bit more influential. It is an old-boy network that has created a revolving door between the firm and public office, greased by the mountains of money the company is generating even today, as its peers buckle and fall. Almost whatever the country, you can find Goldman Sachs veterans in positions of pivotal power."

Once again in the Independent Newspaper, Stephen Foley wrote another article in November 2011 demonstrating how Goldman Sachs is involved in power throughout the world:

"The ascension of Mario Monti to the Italian prime ministership is remarkable for more reasons than it is possible to count. By replacing the scandal-surfing Silvio Berlusconi, Italy has dislodged the undislodgeable. By imposing rule by unelected technocrats, it has suspended the normal rules of democracy, and maybe democracy

itself. And by putting a senior adviser at Goldman Sachs in charge of a Western nation, it has taken to new heights the political power of an investment bank that you might have thought was prohibitively politically toxic. This is the most remarkable thing of all: a giant leap forward for, or perhaps even the successful culmination of, the Goldman Sachs Project.

It is not just Mr Monti. The European Central Bank, another crucial player in the sovereign debt drama, is under ex-Goldman management, and the investment bank's alumni hold sway in the corridors of power in almost every European nation, as they have done in the US throughout the financial crisis. Until Wednesday, the International Monetary Fund's European division was also run by a Goldman man, Antonio Borges, who just resigned for personal reasons."

In this same article, Simon Foley also referred his readers to a book called *'13 bankers: The Wall Street takeover and next Financial Meltdown'* written by Simon Johnson, the former chief economist of the International Monetary Fund and James Kwak who is a Professor of Law at the University of Connecticut School of Law. It was in this book they argued that Goldman Sachs and the other large banks had become so close to government in the run-up to the financial crisis that the US was effectively an oligarchy. At least European politicians aren't "bought and paid for" by corporations, as in the US, he says. "Instead what you have in Europe is a shared world-view among the policy elite and the bankers, a shared set of goals and mutual reinforcement of illusions."

Interestingly, I recall watching an amazing BBC news broadcast several years ago at the beginning of the 2008 Global Debt crisis. It was very amusing to see the news team make the mistake of interviewing a money dealer who pronounced that the world was going to be plunged into chaos. He clearly stated "governments do not rule the world; Goldman Sachs Bank rules the world." He went on to say that he, as a money dealer, was really looking forward to the turmoil because whatever happened to the financial markets, he believed he would make money. Like all money dealers he would, of course, turn this money into real hard, tangible assets that actually existed, like land and property which would have value even if paper money had none because digital money exists only in cyber space and can disappear as fast as it appears in the first place. He stressed that he loved being in such times, but he also said that this would be a time of financial devastation for millions. His less than acceptable moral concern clearly shook the interviewers and seemed to cause such embarrassment that they then endeavoured to make some rather feeble jokes as they tried to get him off the air. However, I believe that, unbeknown to the viewers, he actually stated the reality of the situation in many ways; he was absolutely right about the crisis that followed.

Throughout the New Testament we are warned continually, to keep watch for Jesus' coming and to be ready. We are now at a unique moment in the history of the world as we witness all these signs prophesied in the Bible concerning the end times. As we move into times of severe persecution, we need to be able to stand firm in our faith. We are facing the final stages of history where, as the Bible says, the anti-Christ spirit will increase in power, leading to a time of great falling away from the Christian faith and a time of troubles never before experienced as the great authoritarian power comes to the fore.

The Bible teaches that this will lead to the emergence of the Anti-Christ taking his place in the Temple in Jerusalem, where he will declare himself to be God. Further, that he will rule all people groups throughout the world with great authority but this will lead to mass destruction and turmoil. I believe that church leaders should be urged most strongly to prepare their people for what lies ahead. The final 'Day of the Lord' will bring anguish to millions of people who have refused to heed the signs, but it will bring great joy to those who have been keeping watch and are called by his name.

Chapter 3: The Great Last Days Money Deception

In this chapter, I want to consider how money, debt and trade will play key roles in the final outworking of the authoritarian rule that the Bible says will arise in the last days before Jesus returns.

Many people in the Western world have been deceived into believing an illusion; that health, wealth and happiness are the goals of every human being. That maybe, just maybe, utopia is possible on this earth! This is, after all, the apparent goal of the United Nations initiative called the 2030 Sustainable Development Agenda launched about two years ago. Most countries have already embraced its principles and ideals, and however unlikely it may seem, a target date of 2030 has been set as the point by which this new utopian world is to be achieved. But every utopian dream has always been nothing but an illusion involving deception, leading to authoritarianism. Interestingly, the Bible does speak of such a utopian dream in the future, but it will not be created by man on this earth; it will be a new heaven and a new earth created by God (more on this later).

Western society has, since the end of the Second World War,
experienced considerable economic success. It is principally due to endless supplies of credit, high powered technological progress aided by computerisation and cheap energy (oil) to run its infrastructure. But it has now reached the point where nations are literally drowning in vast amounts of debt, most of which can never be repaid.

The Illusion of Wealth

For those of you who remember the famous 1990s film called *The Mattrix*, you might recall that the main character, played by Keano Reeves, was asked at the beginning if he wanted to take the blue pill and stay in the world of illusion, or the red pill that would plunge him into the world of reality. I believe that this is the exact question everyone living in the Western world should be asking themselves again today. After carrying out research into what happened to cause the 2008 Global Debt Crisis over the last ten years, I believe that the evidence is clear that we have all been living in a kind of 'Mattrix' or Illusion for the past 50/60 years.

This illusion of wealth was created after the end of the Second World War with the creation of a debt-based money system, the full ramifications of which burst into reality in September 2008. Most people have no idea that the creation of such a debt-based money system was originally the brainchild of a small group of international bankers, including the Rothschilds, the Morgans, and the Rockefellers who met in secret at a place called Jekyll Island in the USA shortly after the last great economic crash in 1929. *(The book called 'The Creature from Jekyll Island* by G. Edward Griffin is the most comprehensive report of how this happened)*. This conspiracy to create a money-making system for bankers has in fact enabled us, in the West, to live in the relative comfort that we do today, but it was known that it couldn't last forever.

This illusory bubble actually first started to burst in 1987 with the first World Stock Market Crash that I was personally involved with. Could this event have been predicted and warnings given? Looking back, the answer is most certainly yes. In fact, many people did predict the likelihood of such a happening.

One such person, amongst many, was the Economist Ann Pettifor. She was the founder of what became known as Jubilee 2000 which called for the cancellation of all Third World debt in the year 2000. She managed to get this concept across to many churches and through the pressure of millions of Christians, much of the debt was then actually cancelled by the Gordon Brown government. In her book *'The Coming First World Debt Crisis'*, she recalled that as she flew back from the third world she looked out over the West and realised that the major problem looming was not so much the Third World debt, as bad as it was, but the enormity of First World debt.

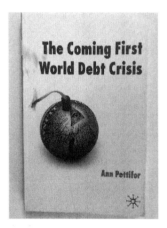

This was one of the very first books that I read in 2008 shortly after its publication in 2006. She identified several reasons as to why the first world debt was likely to implode and why various events could be the trigger. She was right. Of the various likely triggers, it turned out to be the derivatives debt markets in subprime mortgages that imploded in 2007.

It began in the USA and then spread rapidly across the whole of the Western World. Trillions in false wealth had been created out of thin air and wrapped up in packages labelled as securities that were subsequently revealed for what they were – worthless. These securities had been sold to banks across the world rated by the credit agencies as Triple A rated security against loans. They were also sold to pensions funds and thousands of savings vehicles in the same way; all regarded thereafter as real wealth. In reality, they comprised nothing but debt that could disappear in a puff of smoke, which is exactly what happened.

The Great Debt Party

It seemed that the world had literally gone mad, thinking that debt didn't matter and that it wasn't even necessary to try to understand it all because everyone was enjoying a standard of living based entirely on the illusion that debt was OK. Perhaps the greatest illusion occurred when the Access card was introduced in the United Kingdom on 23 October 1972. It was then that a consortium consisting of the National Westminster Bank, the Midland Bank, Lloyds Bank and the National and Commercial Banking Group came together as a rival to the established Barclaycard. Known as 'Credit Cards' the public were persuaded to think that debt was actually credit. They were led to believe that they had a new-found wealth. Since then, personal debt has rocketed and the banks continue to make a fortune from exorbitant rates of interest.

When it came to people's savings, millions had simply believed they just could just leave their hard-earned savings and investments in the hands of those who supposedly did understand the intricacies of the 'money systems', and all would be well. The reaction by thousands of people to the collapse of the banks in the UK following the Lehman Brothers Bank collapse in the US brought home the fact that it was not easy to withdraw personal savings once thought to be safe. People who had been trying to bring warnings about the sheer level of greed were, of course, ignored at the time. The amazing thing, is that these so called 'professionals' who caused the crisis in the first place, were the very ones who were then called upon by governments to fix the problems they had created. Ironically, there was no-one else to call upon, because no-one understood the incredible complication of such an intertwined and complex system. They have since made further fortunes from this system and one wonders what they actually fixed! Before moving on, let's stop for a moment to think about what money really is, because this is a subject most people never think about – they just use it!

What is Money?

The money system has undergone many changes over the last 100 years which makes understanding where money comes from and who produces it very important. During this period, the concept of economic success became synonymous with being wealthy and wealth with having money. But money and wealth are not to the same. People have accepted government propaganda that economic success equals greater wealth but what they don't really clarify, is that such wealth has been based on debt.

Amongst those who study economic theory at school or university, only a few end up in positions of political power as economists with control over the money system. Many economists have, over the years come to regard economics as a science but gradually, people have realised that it is not a science at all; it is simply using a set of mathematical formulas that are supposed to forecast how to control the money supply in line with human behaviour in the light of rising or falling demand for goods and services in order to keep an economy working well. The problem is, no matter how predictable mathematical formulas might be, human behaviour remains unpredictable. Economic forecasting can, in reality, be notoriously inaccurate in the light of this. Over the last 10 years since the Global Debt Crisis, the value and insight of these so-called professional economists has been brought into severe question because many people asked why they didn't see the 2008 crisis coming in the first place. Even the queen is said to have asked this very question to her many personal advisers.

It is undoubtedly true that Western governments are aware of the seriousness of world debt and even the possibility of the debt causing a world-wide monetary collapse. However, media coverage, no doubt highly influenced by 'power' has, since the initial crisis, managed to present the public with confusing mixed messages. As a result, the majority still do not believe or really understand why nations are embroiled in such huge amounts of debt because it has become a way of life for millions of people. But eventually, sooner or later, a further crisis will occur that could quite possibly bring about a monetary collapse and a debt implosion. But this will be the precise set of circumstances needed in order for the world to accept a world leader, able to bring some stability in the midst of chaos. It is, after all, how most dictators and authoritarian governments have come into power throughout history. With total control over the monetary system and the ability to trade, people will be unable to survive unless they can find ways to sustain themselves outside the system. This may sound very dramatic but it is what the scriptures teach during the last days before Jesus returns.

 Put simply, money can be anything but it is principally meant to be a measure by which people can buy and sell goods and services to each other. It is also supposed to conform to certain characteristics and this primarily means limited supply to ensure that it retains value. The amount of money created is also meant to be in line with the amount required to meet supply and demand for goods and services to ensure that prices remain stable. If there were no money, we would be reduced to the barter economy of the past. This was when every item someone wanted to purchase had to be exchanged for something that person could provide. For example, a person wanting a loaf of bread might only have chickens in exchange. They would have to find someone who wanted a chicken and then try to agree how many loaves of bread would be needed to complete the transaction. Clearly this makes trade more difficult because such items are not easily divisible into smaller units. But with money, you can have smaller units and you don't need to find a particular person. You just need a market in which to sell your goods or services. In that

market, you don't barter for individual goods. Instead you exchange your goods or services for a common medium of exchange—that is, money. You can then use that money to buy what you need from others who also accept the same medium of exchange.

What makes defining money more complicated nowadays is that most people do not realise that there is a difference between governments using central banks to produce the currency of the realm in coins or paper money and digital or 'plastic card' type money which is produced by

ordinary main stream banks. This is done when they make loans or provide 'credit' (debt in reality) to ordinary citizens. What is more, the majority of people have no idea where money comes from at all. We have heard it said often enough by politicians that money doesn't grow on trees! You could argue that it does for

them. It should be extremely concerning that in numerous interviews conducted on the streets of various cities around the world, people cannot answer the question, "Do you know where money comes from"? Virtually no one has any idea apart from a fairly common guess, which went along the following lines: 'Does it come from trees?' How is this possible? The answer is quite simple, because they have never had to know. Few people really appreciate the consequences of our lack of understanding.

Even Politicians Don't Know!

What is really concerning is that recent surveys in the UK have revealed that even 9 out of 10 elected politicians have no understanding of what money is or where it comes from either. It is quite unbelievable to think that there has been so little education in our schools or universities about money but this is something I have witnessed first-hand during my working career as a financial adviser. It is clear that this has enabled elitists to maintain power through the creation of our money. It leaves the population clueless about how the money system can be manipulated by central bankers and retail banks leaving people to come to their own, usually wrong, conclusions on the subject.

Money from Nothing!

Creating money out of nothing, started from the old money lenders holding people's gold for them and issuing receipts for the gold that were gradually used in place of the gold and so they became paper money. This meant that people came to trust in using the receipts only as money rather than having to use the gold which they were told was always held safely. This was a complete lie. In time, these money lenders realised that they could simply issue receipts without the need to hold the corresponding amount of gold at all because they believed that not everyone would return to claim their physical gold at the same time. Eventually, they could even lease out gold to other lenders who would issues receipts likewise.

Thus, the modern-day concept of 'Fractional Reserve Banking' was born, i.e. more receipts issued than gold held. Banks today now do the same; issuing up to ten times in loans the amount of deposits held. Thus, they only hold a fraction of the money deposited compared with the amount of loans made longer term. The problems start when people want their money returned all at the same time, when the bank will experience a bank run and need to be bailed out by Governments with taxpayer's money.

Until 1971, money throughout the Western world was backed by gold, which was known as the gold standard. It was possible to go into a bank and demand an amount of gold equivalent to the amount of the paper note and vice versa. For reasons beyond the scope of this book, the gold standard was abandoned in 1971 and the whole world changed to a paper-backed 'Fiat' paper-based system. The word Fiat is Latin 'for let it be' and it means that newly printed money can be produced by central banks whenever they wish. If it is perceived that an economy is failing as happened in 2008 the central banks turn to 'the money-making tree' so to speak to create more liquidity in the system. But this new money is created out of nothing. The belief that paper or digital money has value is based solely on the assumption that Governments will provide a guarantee to honour it. But it must be remembered that governments have no money of their own. They rely on the tax that they receive from the population to uphold this guarantee. If the people can no longer support the level of tax required or produce enough from their work, then the value of this money cannot be sustained. But the more money they pump into the system, the less value it has, for it is diluting the value of previously created money all the time, whilst increasing the level of debt.

Money Equals Debt

Without proper control by governments and central banks, these retail banks can create money at will. This is the situation that has existed in most Western nations for decades. But the money they create actually equals debt. How does this happen? It occurs every time they grant a loan to someone or provide them with credit. They create money literally out of thin air at the touch of a computer button. For example, if a customer were to borrow say £10,000 to buy a car, the bank would create the money on their balance sheet digitally and then credit it to the customer's account. They would then transfer this money at another touch of a button to the dealer's account selling the car. Thus, new money has come into existence. What is not generally known is that when this new money is paid into the dealers account, the receiving bank can then create up to ten times the amount in further loans to their customers and as each new loan is paid into customer accounts each receiving bank is creating a further ten times the amount in even more new loans. This is what is known as 'fractional reserve' banking. Effectively new money, or should I say debt is created in the billions or even trillions, not by governments, but by private banks. *"Let us control the money of a nation, and we care not who makes the law"*. This was said to be the maxim of the House of Rothschild. It is absolutely true and it has been proven to be true over the centuries.

Can World Debt Really be Repaid?

At this stage, I would say this is most unlikely, if not impossible. Whilst politicians speak about their determination to live within their means by reducing debt, most people do not realise that under our present money system, debts can never be repaid without a substantial increase in world growth. This seems most unlikely because most nations are now struggling with reductions in global growth. This means governments can only sustain current spending levels by increasing the level of borrowing. The alternative is to cut public expenditure through austerity measures but it doesn't affect the really wealthy in society. But it looks very much like we are at the end of the road. With world economic growth falling and debt continuing to rise, there is every reason to expect another debt implosion, especially if interest rates are increased. This time, it is highly unlikely governments will be able to use taxpayer's money to bail out a debt-based system as they did in 2008 because further debt can no longer be absorbed.

Private and government debt is now at the highest levels in history. As I have stressed before, this is the key to what is happening. The whole world has been enslaved with debt at every level. Debt is affecting everyone on the planet. Never before have all the Central Banks in the world printed so much money at the same time to keep the main stream banks from going under. Have the banks learned anything from this disaster? Not really. They have since gone on to create any number of highly questionable financial products using mathematical algorithms, high speed trading of assets and derivatives that make them vastly rich at the expense of their unsuspecting customers.

The Global Debt Crisis of 2008 was entirely due to gross mismanagement of debt by banks, financial regulators and politicians and it brought the whole world's monetary system to within an hour of complete collapse. It was the world's worst debt implosion ever known. Suddenly, the banking system was exposed to the fact that it's supposed assets were nothing more packages of debt wrapped up to look like valuable securities, against which, loans were made. Once it was discovered that these securities were worthless, the banks liquidity ceased up. Had the monetary system collapsed, the effects would have brought Western societies to a grinding halt and caused social chaos.

We saw an example of what happens when banks cease up when people formed long queues outside the Northern Rock only to find that they could not withdraw any of their savings. This forced the UK government to declare that it would provide guarantees (backed by public taxes) to prevent a total run on the bank. We saw it happen in Greece a few years ago, when banks were declared insolvent and they closed for over two weeks. No-one could access their savings apart from small amounts of cash from ATM cash dispenser machines each day. People struggled to obtain sufficient money to buy food, clothing or medicines. Few people have any idea how close the world came to this type of chaos in 2008. This was when suddenly, the world came face to face with the reality of living in a debt-based money system where the value of all assets is totally unconnected to real value. It was when people realised that our savings are only represented by digits on a balance sheet and we are not free to easily withdraw the money in the event of a banking insolvency. Until that point, people in the Western world had been under the illusion that they could carry on with their seemingly normal lives without understanding the consequences of a debt-based money system

But these are signs of things still to come. The truth is that this near global catastrophe was only averted because governments and central banks began to print trillions of newly printed monies in an attempt to prop up a disintegrating system. It was meant to be for a short period, probably no more than 6 months during this emergency, but it has now been carried on for over ten years and the debt is now double the 2008 figure. This 'oiling of the system' with even more debt has given the impression that our world economies have somehow returned to normal and are thriving once again, when all the while, they are living on more and more debt. It is similar to, but not exactly the same, to families who take out debt on credit cards that need to be repaid by new credit cards until, eventually, the credit card companies realise that the debt cannot be repaid and refuse to issue any more cards.

Meanwhile, the banks have had to comply with new rules that supposedly provides the public with greater protection in the event of any future banking collapse. In reality, these rules have ensured that certain categories of highly favoured investors (known as derivative holders) with potential liabilities in the trillions will be considered first, over and above ordinary deposit holders, like you and me. The enormity of these potential liabilities virtually guarantees the loss of these deposits in the event of a future bank insolvency.

The Key to Control

We know from the Bible that money and the monetary system, will probably play the greatest role in the climax of events taking place in the last days. It teaches that the love of money (mammon = wealth) is the root of all evil and that over time, people, in seeking their own success and love for money and the wealth it can provide, will gradually fall away from believing in the God of the Bible. Instead, in seeking to reach new heights of glory, their love for money, wealth and power will cause them to stumble; their dreams and visions for the future failing, eventually leading to chaos. As this chaos increases, it tells us that in the midst of this euphoria and greed, a new world leader will arise and be welcomed. This will presumably be because of his charismatic appeal, confidence and ability to control the entire world's monetary system; he will bring about the appearance of stability for a period of time. It says that this man will wield unheard of power, because, in controlling the whole world's monetary system, he will also be able to prevent everyone on the earth from being able to transact (buy or sell) without his authority. Those who are unwilling to obey his edicts will find themselves his enemy, unlikely to survive. As amazing as it may seem, this precise scenario was prophesied in the Bible over 2,000 year ago. The Bible calls this new world ruler the Anti-Christ (means in place of Christ) and prophesies that he will arise using very advanced technology highly likely to not only monitor every split-second money transaction taking place across the whole earth, but to also track the whereabouts of every citizen on the earth.

This might seem like some giant conspiracy theory or science fiction story to many people, but if the ancient scriptures are to be believed, we are faced with this reality, like it or not. But the Bible also says that this situation is not going to materialise without many signs first having appeared well ahead of time that will bring an awareness and a warning to prepare for what lies ahead. Only those who are prepared to study the scriptures and gain an awareness of how economic, political, technological and ecological events are converging and gathering momentum, will be able to 'join the dots' and see the 'wood for the trees'.

We have now reached the stage where the level of technological progress has advanced to the point whereby such control could actually be implemented which I discuss in the chapter on Technology. In addition, the globalist agenda that has dominated politics for many decades is in its last stages of its implementation. Using threats of terrorism, mass immigration, climate change and nuclear war, people can easily be persuaded, with little personal research, to join this globalist agenda because they are being convinced that the continuation of life on earth is at stake! Never before in human history have we arrived at the point whereby it has become possible to recognise most of the signs prophesied in the Bible that speak of the rise of this world leader followed by the second coming of Jesus Christ.

Cash – The Last Bastion of Independence

The use of cash as money is quite likely the last bastion in being able to buy and sell whilst maintaining complete anonymity, although the sudden launch of many crypto-currencies like Bitcoin do claim to achieve this as well. The idea of dissuading the population from using cash as money is clearly a major part of the globalist plan towards obtaining total control. This usually involves constant references in the media to cash being used by money launderers and terrorists. The final

coup de grâce comes when government tells us that doing away with cash will ensure it is more effective in preventing tax evasion. All of this is rather strange when you realise that only 3% of money in circulation is cash. The remaining 97% of money used in Western society is already digital and subject to total control. Extinguishing cash from the system will achieve their aim of total control. From a globalist point of view however, over 40% of the world's population still does not have access to banking facilities and relies on cash. It is clear that mobile technology is already being developed to accommodate this large sector in order to completely dispense with cash (more on this later in the technology section).

Many people will therefore ask, how close are we to the establishment of this authoritarian form of control? The answer, is a lot closer than most people think. It is clearly not possible to give dates or times but the Bible does say we can know the seasons when we can expect these things to occur. I believe that it is clear that we are now in the midst of this season because all the last day signs prophesied in the Bible are being revealed. As we draw close to its implementation we should expect what all controlling regimes do; introduce a time of confusion and unrest within society to divert people's attention away from what is really happening. A further financial crisis could do just the job!

Never Mind - We are all in it together!

The reality is that the world is now sitting on an even bigger, ever looming debt time bomb and the coming catastrophe that can be expected has been turned into something much bigger. The day of reckoning still awaits us! With Western governments having bailed out the banks with tax payers' money and passing the costs of their mistakes to the public, the banks have subsequently become even richer and the public poorer. When the former Prime Minister David Cameron said, *'We are all in it together'*, the truth was that the elites avoided the calamity and the public took the full force of the disaster. Since then, the liabilities are now coming to the point when the reality of low or even no growth will impact people's savings once again and we will see millions of people finding pension promises made years ago from both government and private schemes that cannot be met. What do you think this will cause people to do this time around? This time, the Central Banks have run out of tools (the creation of even more debt) to deal with another crisis and the debt has doubled to epidemic proportions. The world has never seen a situation like this before.

So, has the problem been fixed? The answer is no. Yes, the world financial meltdown was temporarily alleviated in 2008 through government intervention using a range of financial 'tools' including the use of financial derivatives and mathematical algorithms, but the governments and central banks have once again shifted the implications to the general public and passed laws that allow those who created the disaster in the first place, the banks, to escape liability.

Let's face it - the World is in a mess!

Converging Signs and Rejection of Truth

Ambassador Wolfgang Ischinger has been Chairman of the Munich Security Conference since 2008 and in his opening speech in 2018, he stated that the world was in a mess. But we are now in an even larger mess than in 2008. (Go to You Tube to hear this speech). Many people believe that the money printing policies have done the trick, because the bankers and news media tell us so! We are also led to believe that Western economies are beginning to thrive again. This may appear correct at first glance. But if we 'look under the bonnet', so to speak, at the real state of investments and values across the world, we will see nothing but devastation. For example, the values of pension funds are propped up by the actuaries' forecasts based on ancient investment models with expectations and assumptions of average annual growth rate of about 7% to 8%, taking account of the usual spread of investments across so-called risk categories. These values no longer represent reality. Pension funds haven't, as a rule, experienced anything like this growth for years and years. Every three years, these funds have to be assessed and valued and we are now entering into reality as it is being discovered that liabilities far exceed assets which will result in the need to change previously agreed pension promises. The outcomes will bring much disappointment and even misery to millions of people who will see their pensions cut severely from those originally promised.

The truth is, that rising world debt is in the process of causing a massive implosion within our societies. The perceived values of all traditional savings have been warped beyond recognition. Every type of investment vehicle has been affected. Government bonds, corporate bonds, equities both UK and International and of the course the highly overvalued property markets. With world GDP continuing to contract, there is no chance of these funds being able to meet their liabilities. All the while, people in the West have lived in relative comfort but under the illusion that had led us to believe our money represented wealth. It has been a hard lesson to learn that money is in reality nothing other than a piece of paper that can disappear with the click of a mouse on the computer of a bank.

Whose should be held Accountable?

The faults in the system that caused this crisis have not been fixed. How many Bankers or 'Banksters', as many now call them, have been brought to account? How many regulators? How many politicians? Has anything changed for the better? Whilst regulators try to tell us how much better shape the International Banks are now in, the reality is that the systemic problems that existed are as bad, if not worse. Why? Because the 'elitist culture' still exists and has no interest in hearing the voices of the people whose lives have been ruined over the past ten years as a result of the extreme policies that were introduced to favour the big banks following the 2008 Global crisis. By having control of money creation, the elitists, governments and banks have been able to manipulate the value of everything in the financial markets to their own advantage and hundreds of billions is made in profit no matter whether the markets go up or down. The only ones to lose are the general public. These elitists have become the truly wealthy of our world whilst the rest of the population has become poorer. It is estimated by Oxfam, for example, in their latest annual survey, that 62 families in the world control over 50% of the entire worlds wealth. Also, that *1%of the world has taken 82% of all the wealth in 2017.*

The Final Collapse of the Monetary System – But When?

 We are now looking at the biggest asset to debt bubble values ever blown in history. A collapse of the world's monetary system will have consequences for societies too enormous to contemplate. 'Fiat', or paper money has no worth if the faith that it can continue to be honoured is lost. This is the fate for the future of paper money that we are looking at in the future. The biggest problem, however, is not knowing when this will happen. In reality, it is actually happening all the time as Central Banks continue to print digital money, the real value of which, decreases in our pockets every day. They will continue to do so until they literally can't print anymore or the balloon pops! Then, the game is over! We have been duped into believing that life, as we now know it, can continue, but this is a serious illusion and a direct lie. Never before has the world ever

found itself in such a situation. Never before have millions of people been so deceived by images of a future that cannot turn into reality. Never before has the entire world been deceived and deluded into thinking that it can continue to survive on debt and living beyond our means.

I believe that a time is coming when government and central bank mechanisms will be unable to uphold such a corrupt operation and this will lead to an implosion of debt right across the financial system. This will be unlike anything the world has ever experienced and it will be of such intensity that everything about money and the money system will change beyond recognition. The likely outcome will involve the re-evaluation of all 'digital' assets i.e. paper values, which will mean significant reductions in perceived value as currently understood. People will be 'shell shocked'. We all need to remember that governments and banks have had 10 years to deal with the implications of the debt implosion of 2008 and yet their only solution has been to carry on with business as usual; allowing it to increase continually. We are literally becoming the debt slaves to a technological society that is, in reality, all part of the great deception.

The scene is being set for the rise of the final authoritarian centralised monetary system to operate and we should, by now, have a much better understanding of how it will enable the Anti-Christ authoritarian ruler to gain control over people's ability to buy and sell. Let's now consider the political signs .

Chapter 4: Political Signs

Over the past ten years or so, a kind of rebellion has risen up with millions of ordinary people from all political persuasions saying that they are fed-up with those who have wielded political power over them. Ordinary people throughout the West are being prevented from being able to express an opinion without being immediately condemned or vilified. It is affecting the human spirit, creating disunity and anger and even hate within families and various people groups. Politicians are making decisions that result in laws that have been sought after by only a tiny minority and yet they affect the majority.

All the world's 'systems' that we have been living under and taken for granted for decades are being shaken. The ground is shaking so to speak, beneath our feet leaving people bewildered and unable to see where it is all leading. We are witnessing continued aggression between the West and the East battling over the worlds diminishing resources with the expected clashes between the major powers as they try to establish their so-called values and perceived rights. How could so many, seemingly unconnected, events be happening on a such a wide scale that create so much insecurity? Many say that powerful 'elites' are behind it all and to some extent this is true. However, these 'elites' from all parts of the world are not able to act in unison with the exact same intentions and the Bible tells us that there is actually only one 'spirit' driving it. The spirit of the *'kingdom of the air'* – the spirit of the anti-Christ. Some may laugh at those believing in such things because it is perceived that we are all so much more sophisticated in this modern scientific age. However, for millions of ordinary people caught in the middle of the mayhem, fear and uncertainty is all there is and whatever people may believe, the fact is that there are millions of Christians in the world who know that spiritual forces are real and leading to a unique moment in history which the Bible speaks very clearly about.

Israel '- God's Time Piece'

It is often said that Israel is God's timepiece that will enable us to become aware of how close we are to the end times described in the scriptures. Watching events taking place throughout the Middle East, particularly in Israel provides a clearer understanding of the times. Although the Middle East always appears to be in the news for one reason or another, we are today witnessing enormous changes and threats to peace. We are literally watching ancient prophecies in the Bible coming true in our day with mass uprising amongst the peoples and the threats being made towards Israel by Iran, whose leaders have openly and consistently stated that they *"want to wipe Israel off the face of the earth."* We see Turkey, a member of the NATO alliance, with President Recep Tayyip Erdogan fresh from his controversial election, appearing to view himself as the chosen successor of a revived Ottoman empire, the Sultan of a new Islamic caliphate. More worryingly, we have now seen over 128 countries in the United Nations recently voting to condemn the decision by the US to locate the US Embassy in Jerusalem as the recognised capital of Israel. Congress took the decision to move the US Embassy from Tel Aviv to Jerusalem in the 1990s but Trump's predecessors failed to implement the law. Although everyone agrees that any country has the right to decide its own capital city, most people have little understanding of the reasons why President Trump's decision should cause such uproar. Why all the fuss about little old Israel, one of the smallest countries in the whole world? Once again, the Bible provides the answers.

In the meantime, major uprisings are taking place in Iran as the people try to free themselves from the religious leader's grip. This is the country whose leadership speaks of the USA the 'Great Satan' and of Israel as the 'Little Satan'.

At the latest World Security conference in Munch in 2018, Benjamin Netanyahu, the Prime Minister of Israel, praised President Trump's decision to locate the US Embassy in Jerusalem as one of the greatest events in history since the Balfour declaration, 100 years ago, when England was blessed by God for taking the action they did in recognising Israel as a State. He then announced that Israel would take action against any further moves by Iran to build military forces near its borders. It would be so encouraging to see Christian leaders proclaiming the importance of this event in accordance with the Biblical and prophetic last day 'signs', but instead, we mainly see silence and indifference and, often criticism of Israel from within the church. It is unfortunate that so few Christian leaders seem to understand the significance of the real struggle between Israel and the 'Palestinians' or even why the 'Jerusalem' decision is so important in term of Biblical prophecy.

The Bible says that a time will come when all the nations of the world will turn against Israel and we are now witnessing the latest decision by the British, French and German governments calling for this Jerusalem declaration decision to be renounced. This raises serious questions about any blessing we may think God will bring today to the UK. But the Bible also says that when the nations do turn against Israel, God will miraculously come to their rescue. Are these things not what we should be teaching in our churches today about the times in which we live?

The Rise of Islam

In the midst of all this confusion, the confrontations across the Middle East, which are especially pronounced in Syria and Yemen had resulted in Inter Islamic warfare between Shia and Sunni Muslims. Muslims are being displaced in their millions and migrating towards Europe. Few of these displaced people go to other more stable Arab countries. Once again, it is likely that this has Biblical significance as well. International Bible teacher David Pawson, has prophesied that the UK will become a Muslim nation within the next ten years! How could this happen? Quite simply when you realise how many children they have compared to Western people who abort many of theirs! In his book *"The Challenge of Islam to Christians"* written in 2003, the introduction says: *"The Challenge of Islam to Christians is David Pawson's most important - and most controversial - prophetic message to date. Moral decline and erosion of a sense of ultimate truth has created a spiritual vacuum in the United Kingdom. David Pawson believes Islam is far better equipped than the Church to move into that gap and it will not be long before it becomes the country's dominant religion"*

Converging Signs and Rejection of Truth

In various You-Tube presentations, David Pawson has gone further and said that he believes this could be the hand of God bringing judgment on our land, using Muslims just as he used the Babylonians to bring judgement against the Jews who had turned their backs on God. Is this not concerning? Does this not cause us to stand up and say - NO? Does it not call for church leaders to cry out to God in repentance and ask for forgiveness?

But this mass immigration of Muslims into Europe brings with it a completely different 'spirit'. It is proving to be a very controversial issue and one that is causing huge problems for European countries which, apart from Germany, are drowning in massive amounts of debt and now have new added financial pressures to supply homes, food, schools, healthcare, employment, etc. The effects on the Western culture cannot fail to be profound trying to integrate people with a completely different attitude and belief system. Anyone should be able to see clearly the rise of Islam becoming a major concern in the western world. Whilst many will proclaim that it is only fundamentalist Islam with which we need to be concerned, it should be obvious that the teachings of the Koran are contrary to those of the Christian faith. The Koran states, that Allah has no son and that Jesus was only a prophet: it is blasphemy to regard Jesus as God incarnate. It proclaims that Allah is the only true One God; the Trinity is blasphemy. These differences alone demonstrate that Islam is incompatible with Christianity; both religions do not worship the same God. However, it appears that very few church leaders are willing to expose the major differences that exist between the Christian faith and Islam. Chaos and conflict is inevitable and as with all conflict, appeasement and negotiation is not always the right approach. *[This is not a subject for further comment in this book, because there are numerous sources that can provide deeper understanding on this matter].* However, this rise of Islam, which we are clearly seeing, is seriously impacting Europe with people whose values are nothing like Western values originally based on the Judeo and Christian scriptures as well as the teachings of Jesus Christ who proclaimed himself to be God. The impact is obvious for those people with eyes to see. The intensity of this infiltration can only get worse with the rise of far-right parties in Austria, Germany and Hungry.

The United Kingdom and Europe

Throughout Europe we see those in power trying to maintain their control over the people as they move towards the authoritarian rule endeavouring to bring all nations under fiscal control. We also see the plans still on the table to create a European Military force. This is all part of the great move towards what many people see as an attempt to establish a One World System where 'equality' is the main ideology.

Since the referendum on the UK's future relationship with the EU, there has continued to be huge disagreement with those who believe the

Converging Signs and Rejection of Truth

UK should remain part of the European Union and those who wish us to leave. The 'leavers' want the UK to take back it's laws and to have control over immigration. The 'remainers' believe the EU was set up to avoid future wars and to maintain trade with our European partners and to secure jobs. Many young people simply view the need to remain in the EU as a means of being able to travel and study without boarder restrictions. It is remarkable how few see, or even care about, the underlying desire for total unification under one rule. As a result, we now see the 'tug-of-war' between politicians with opposing views about Brexit involving the various attempts to reverse the Brexit decision and undermining the referendum.

It is not really surprising to see such a struggle, because this is, in my opinion, and the opinion of many others, the attempt by globalists to keep the United Kingdom in a non-democratic union that continues to move steadily towards its utopian authoritarian' rule.

Converging Signs and Rejection of Truth

The United States of America

Here we see a gigantic battle for the continuation of the rule of law and democracy. However, we need to remember that in reality it is all about the power of the trans-global corporations controlling the politicians through the power of money. We are now witnessing politicians, the CIA, the FBI as well as the mainstream media appearing to do everything that they can to

discredit and dislodge President Trump, whether by personal slurs or by often totally unfounded and false allegations. Never before have we seen such an onslaught of both love and hate towards a President of the USA. It is extremely difficult for the man in the street to weigh up the pros and cons of the arguments. However, we can see from news reports that there is a great deal of reaction amongst people in positions of power following his 'draining the swamp' promises during his election campaign.

Whatever is the truth, it is clear that the American public are finding it very hard to know who can be trusted to act in the interests of the common people and this was the precise issue highlighted during the 2016 Trump presidential election campaign. It was during this period that Trump accused what he considered to be 'The Deep State' (a kind of shadow power opposing government) of attempting to prevents his election. The Democrats including Hilary Clinton then accused Trump of collusion with the Russians and this is still the main thrust of their attack against his presidency. Trump himself recently tweeted 'Would you rather be friends with Russia or go to war'? Furthermore, he accused the main stream press of collusion with this 'deep state' and the term 'fake news' became widely used. Subsequently this term began to be used on a wider basis by other former government officials including Dr Paul Craig Roberts who was the Assistant Treasury Secretary to the Regan administration and former Assistant Editor of the Washington Journal. He and many other 'alternative media' networks, authors and news correspondents also began to report that the deep state was a reality in shaping public opinion.

Another major point of contention concerns governments rights to invade public privacy, especially when issues of terrorism and fraud are being investigated. But whatever you believe, it is clear that President Trump is facing an onslaught of political power against him and only time will decide what information comes out in the public interests and the effect it has on the voting population. Whatever the politics behind all that is going on, the US is still in serious debt that is increasing exponentially. Whilst it is able to print money at no cost to itself using the World's reserve currency, all other currencies are benchmarked against the Dollar. If any country wants to move outside this system, they are usually brought back into line by the US by one means or another. Such is the importance of being able to print endless dollars to keep their economy afloat. In the book by John Perkins called *'Confessions of an Economic Hit Man'*, it is interesting to note his comments about how the US government and their central intelligence agencies function. Perkins writes about how the US seeks to gain access to local resources, often at the expense of the people, all in the name of democracy and maintenance of the all-powerful US dollar and of course 'the common good'. Many are now hopeful that despite the political, public and media reactions to the 'Trump' phenomenon, he is actually managing to enact policies that were promised to the people during his election.

Wars - Nuclear Confrontation?

The world also draws ever closer to nuclear confrontation on several fronts as we see negotiations taking place between major nuclear powers that continue to provoke each other. The reality is that the US is threatened by countries like Russia building its military forces and China growing into a world beating economy. The recent debacle with North Korea seems to have quietened down for the time being but trade wars between China and the US are still reported as an ongoing concern. China may have high levels of internal debt, but unlike the West and particularly the US, its debt has been created through a Public Banking structure which is designed to correspond to the development of their infrastructure. The US has openly admitted that its own infrastructure is now archaic and dilapidated and it seems that the problem of US indebtedness will get worse, with presumably more and more money constantly needed to not only fix the infrastructure but to fight wars all over the globe. However, the Trump Administration now appears to be presenting policies that are designed to rectify these deficiencies and President Trump is calling for NATO countries to increase their spending as he doesn't want the US to continue to take the strain of funding the globalist approach to world affairs.

At the annual Munich World Leaders Security Conference in 2018, it became clear how delicate the world is balanced between major conflict that could easily turn nuclear. The 'war mongering' talk comes not only from the US Congress towards China and Russia, but latterly from the Europe and UK. Despite the rhetoric coming from the media with a bias towards Western supremacy, President Putin has over the last couple of years been trying to bring warnings to the West about their unproven accusations that are constantly made towards his leadership. The politics involved over Russia's involvement in the Ukraine and Crimea are too complicated to discuss in this book. But clearly, war is still on the horizon and the Bible says there will be a rise in power from 'the north' that will come against Israel and many people believe that Russia and China will be those who form this enormous power.

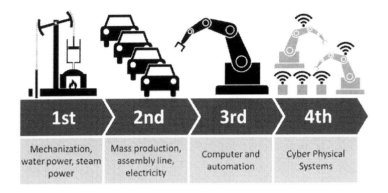

1st	2nd	3rd	4th
Mechanization, water power, steam power	Mass production, assembly line, electricity	Computer and automation	Cyber Physical Systems

Chapter 5: Technological Signs

In this section, I want to provide a broad appraisal of the effect that technology is having on the world and on each of us as individuals.

Everything is speeding up, but this time, we seem to be ready for 'warp speed', a term that was heard from Star Trek fans that considered themselves to be 'Trekkies'. Those who remember these films will recall Captain Kirk ordering the crew to prepare for warp speed. The space ship Enterprise then suddenly switched its engines to develop power that simply made it disappear into the stars in a split second. Technology is developing at 'warp speed' right before our eyes and we had better get used to what it will mean for our future.

We are now facing what can only be described as an onslaught of rapid change. It is being openly admitted by those responsible for this change, that millions of people who were not previously affected, are likely to face huge levels of unemployment and the need for retraining. The problem is, that the new tech related jobs will really only be open to the younger generation who are familiar with computer technology. In addition, artificial intelligence, combined with the development of Robotisation, is looking to totally change everything we understand about the nature of our work.

The 4th Industrial Revolution

Apart from the signs happening in the natural, we have, over the last few centuries seen the world move through three major Industrial revolutions. The first was mechanisation that involved water and steam power. The next involved the introduction of electricity which involved the introduction of mass production through the assembly line. Then came the age of the computer and automation. The latest is now upon us; it has been termed the 4th Industrial Revolution as it is the fourth major industrial era since the initial Industrial Revolution of the 18th century. It is characterised by a fusion of technologies that is blurring the lines between the physical, digital, and biological spheres. It also has 'spiritual' overtones and intensions. It is marked by emerging technological breakthroughs in a number of fields including, robotics, artificial intelligence, nanotechnology, quantum computing, biotechnology, the Internet of Things, 3D printing, autonomous vehicles, etc. Like those before it, this revolution is bringing disruption, but this time, it is affecting almost every industry in every country. The breadth and depth of these changes herald the transformation of entire systems of production, management, and governance. It is being hailed as something that will change everything we thought we knew about the world. All those involved deem this to be a great advance for mankind, but the Bible tells us once again that it will herald the time when mankind will become ruled by such technology. It is such technology that will lead us towards outcomes prophesied in the Bible.

We are in the early stages of this new age of technological and biological integration with computerisation. Amongst the hundreds of people involved, at the heart of such changes, are Elon Musk of Tesla fame and Ray Kurzwell, the Director of Engineering at Google. Kurzwell has enormous influence, particularly on the younger generation. He is a public advocate for the future of transhumanism and gives public talks to share his optimistic outlook on life extension, the future of nanotechnology, robotics and biotechnology. He and other futurists are currently preparing for the fusion of man and machine in the next few years. This, they suggest, will require the building of technology that will enable the Internet of Things to function (more on this later).

Some, mainly technophobes, believe that this is the most exciting time to be alive, but for others, it is already becoming quite frightening. Millions of people are deeply worried about the potential consequences. However, the fact that these new technologies will also enable every person on earth to be tracked 24/7 seems to be accepted across society with remarkably little real resistance. It is even more concerning that so few people seem to question WHO will be doing the tracking. The question is, why do so few people seem to concern themselves with this important detail?

The Data Revolution

 It is becoming clearer that there is a great battle taking place concerning data. In the midst of all this technological development and integration, huge amounts of private data have already been collected by organisations like Facebook, Google, Amazon, Twitter and many other social media groups over the years. When these social media sites were originally launched, people were so excited with the new technologies which allow everyone to easily share information with each other, that they unwittingly shared personal data that was capable of being seen, shared and used by others. We also now realise, that as a result of the latest Facebook debacle, involving the British company Cambridge Analytics where data was harvested without authority, this is probably common practice. I wonder how many of us ever read the dozens of pages of terms and conditions that these social media sites require before signing up? How many of us were aware, for example, that when we were given, free of charge, an email address by organisations like Google, or Microsoft, that the offer had strings

attached? Yet, looking back, with the benefit of hindsight, why would we have thought that we were being given something for nothing? By providing free emails, these groups gained access to vast amounts of free data that could be used for no end of purposes. That was their intention.

We now learn that organisations like the NSA (US National Security Agency) collate vast amounts of such data, the content of every single email can be read by third parties. This accumulation of mass data has been very useful to huge corporations and government and even more so when we consider just how many billions of personal photographs have been added to the data already in their possession.

We are now aware that Google and You Tube and numerous other organisations now use computer algorithms to look at material and decide whether it conforms to their standards. They can simply cut someone off from their site if they consider the content is unsuitable. When Donald Trump accused main stream media of printing 'Fake News' just before being elected as President, he was attacked by every media source, despite many prominent people agreeing that this was fake news. However, in the weeks that followed, the mainstream news outlets began to state that they were going to root out all fake news. However, this then led to many alternative news networks, writers and broadcasters having their own channels branded as 'fake' followed by the closure of what was considered unsuitable material. It was through the huge amounts of data and the power of computer algorithms that machines were able to decide whose material could be published and whose would be stopped. Data has become the most valuable source of wealth for these new organisations. But who decides what is and is not suitable?

Smart Technology

What about so-called 'Smart Technology'? When 'Smart' Televisions were first introduced, few people realised that cameras were installed that could relay personal information and conversations directly to unknown organisations. When 'Smart' mobile phones were introduced, few people realised just how much power they held in their hands or how even their personal conversations could also be relayed to unknown sources. Now, thousands of people are willingly inviting more hungry data searching machines like 'Amazon Echo' or 'Google Home' directly into their homes. These machines allow you to speak to them and they answer back.

But there is more than meets the eye with smart mobile phones. Interestingly, a recent BBC Panorama programme called *'Smartphones: The Dark Side'* has revealed some disturbing facts. As the programme began, the commentator stated that mobile smart phone technology is the world's largest behavioural experiment ever known. This should be clearly disturbing because no-one knows what the eventual outcome will be.

Converging Signs and Rejection of Truth

The main concern that so many people have had over the past few years, has been finding ways to extract this adored little device from what appears to have become an extension of our hands. Everywhere you look, you can see people walking along with their phone in hand either texting, checking emails, typing messages or having conversations that would once have been held in private. So many people no longer speak to each other in restaurants, they eat with one hand with their eyes glued to their smart phone screens. Meanwhile, their children do the same as they keep in constant communication with their peer group on social media or play games. It has become a national problem concerning issues of mental health and even suggestions of brain cancer.

The greatest revelation of the Panorama programme was when the founding president of Facebook stated that their developers admitted the software was designed to create addiction. By employing top psychologists and other professionals in human behaviour, they ensured that the public would become addicted but they still launched it to an unsuspecting world. The programme indicated that all other social media groups, Twitter for example follow the same lines. Perhaps the most disturbing element was when they confirmed through research that these smart phone applications are creating addictions comparable with any other class A drug with all the health implications.

Mobile Money

Converging Signs and Rejection of Truth

One of the most important uses for the smartphone, is its ability to effectively be a bank in our hands. It seems that in virtually no time at all, the technology has become so advanced that people can now carry out banking transactions at the touch of a figure whilst having a meal in a restaurant, or anywhere else for that matter. With applications that have become easier and easier to operate, mobile technology now enables people to make banking transactions in seconds instead of waiting in queues in bank branches. As a result, many banks are closing their branches to save costs.

Clearly, members of the public who have little technological knowledge, who live in remote places and rely on their bank, find this very difficult to cope with. However, no matter how we may view smartphone development, there is no getting away with the fact that it is here to stay. It is through this device that people are going to be able to make monetary transactions between each other faster than anyone can imagine. All the time, this little technological little wonder machine is becoming a means of making transactions that we can't do without. At the same time, it is becoming the means by which centralised control will be able to track our every movement and our every money transaction. The next obvious step, that is actually being tested by many companies, is to integrate this technology into our bodies where we won't need to remember personal passwords or usernames – it will be in our DNA! If and when this is achieved, we will be at the point that allows complete authoritarian control over people's whereabouts and their ability to buy and sell to each other.

The future we may have envisaged is rapidly changing beyond our ability to comprehend it. The integration of all forms of technology during the 4th Industrial Revolution will, I believe, play a major part in the lead up to the rise of the world authoritarian government the Bible refers to.

The Internet

It must be remembered that the Internet, the last major technological revolution, was only really introduced to the masses in the late 1990s when people first thought it was simply 'geeky'. As with previous technological revolutions, only a few could understand the potential, most ordinary people simply couldn't get to grips with it or understand what it really was or what it might even be used for. Many thought it simply unnecessary because of the technology that already existed. Some asked, why use email when we already have an instant fax machine? It is fascinating to watch television interviews from the mid to late 1980s before the Internet began to be used on any major scale with people like *Bill Gates of Microsoft and Steve Jobs of Apple computers as they tried to explain the Internet and its use in the future.* The interviewers so often just smiled at both of them and even made jokes as if they were really geeky people professing geeky ideas. Only a few could see what they saw coming in the future.

The same thing happened with the invention of the train and car, just as it has done over the centuries with any major technological revolution. Initially, and ironically, people thought the car was only successful in the first instance because of  the tyres. They completely overlooked the unseen engine beneath the bonnet and its capacity. Even then, the authorities insisted that people needed to walk in front of these new deadly pieces of technology with a red flag to ensure that they wouldn't kill anyone.

In 1865, Britain introduced the *Locomotives on Highways Act*. Better known as the *Red Flag Act*. The act stipulated that all mechanically powered road vehicles must:

- Have three drivers.
- Not exceed 4mph (6.4 kph) on the open road and 2 mph (3.2kph) in towns.
- Be preceded by a man on foot waving a red flag to warn the public

Converging Signs and Rejection of Truth

In 1896, it was withdrawn and the speed limit increased to 14 mph, therefore taking 31 years to go from 4 mph to 14 mph. This must have been so frustrating for the inventors who knew full well the capacity and purpose of the mechanical vehicle. But, the age of the car matured, as did every other technological revolution before it. Cars were here to stay and, eventually changed transportation for humans.

However, changes due to the Internet revolution took a mere twenty years. Now, over 40% of everyone on the planet relies on the Internet in one way or another. Government, big business, banking and Multinational Corporations have all integrated it with everything we now do. In fact, no one could even operate or communicate without it. Without the Internet, business and life as we now know it would simply grind to a halt. At present, many of the poorer nations have only limited Internet access but the intention is to extend access by some truly new technology. Meanwhile, the rest of the world now uses the Internet almost without thinking. But the next stage is now here.

The 'Internet of Things'

With the Fourth Industrial Revolution being all about the integration of new technologies like Artificial Intelligence (AI) with Robotics, the aim of the Internet of Things is to ensure that these technologies become seamless or invisible to our human awareness in their future use. The intention is that the public will not even realise they are connected to the Internet during their daily use. The Internet of Things will allow not only people but 'things' to communicate with each other, 24 hours a day. It will transact behind the scenes in such a way that we won't even think about it anymore. This will bring huge challenges practically, emotionally and morally. Robotics fused with Artificial Intelligence operating through the Internet. How many ordinary people are going to be able to keep up with such continuing change? Once again, this technology takes us nearer to the time when, because everything happens automatically, we will need to ask ourselves, how much will we be in control?

RFID Technology – Will You be Chipped?

In moving towards totally invisible, streamlined communication, the 'Internet of Things' introduces the concept whereby every 'thing' will be recognisable on the Internet as well. Our houses will be filled with all kinds of gadgets and ordinary everyday consumer goods, from washing machines, to fridges, heating systems and cars and even our clothing embedded with minute RFID (Radio Frequency Identification) chips no bigger than a dot on the page of a book.

But such technology is also being implanted into humans. As previously mentioned, there are more reports each day of people agreeing to having minute chips, the size of a grain of rice, injected into their hands. The reasons, range from hospitals being able to gain complete access to your whole medical history, to tracking a lost family member suffering from dementia, to being able to access everything in the workplace, from entrance doors, to stationery cupboards and of course all technological equipment. The reasons for implanting such chips into a person's hand can therefore sound very appealing, but the fact is, placing such a tracking device into your body is not only highly intrusive, but also sinister in its longer-term intentions. This is because it is likely to bring a gradual and wider acceptance of the technology that will eventually connect the human body directly to the Internet physically. This will allow everyone to be identified and tracked wherever they are in the world and prevent privacy. People do not realise that this technology has been known and used to some extent for the past 60 years already and people are already accepting its implanting into the body.

The intention is that people will no longer have to worry or even realise that the Internet is part of their lives. They won't need to log in to a computer as they do now. They will simply have the access code in their bodies that allows automatic connection 24 hours a day. To achieve this, implants in our bodies are becoming more and more acceptable. People are already inviting such technology because we live in an age where it is the number one addiction and every new idea is invited into our lives. It seems such a fun thing or as the younger generation say 'it is really cool'. Millions will do so and what is more, they will be sold the idea that it is a must for security purposes and for health reasons that will seem so appealing and sensible.

What is the Blockchain?

As a major part of this new revolution, the latest development called Blockchain technology has been added to the list of growing methods of communication that will further change everything we know on the Internet. The Blockchain, also called 'Distributed Ledger Technology', allows transactions to take place on the Internet on a peer-to-peer basis without any middlemen. Its potential is far reaching and its original inventor, said to be Satoshi Nakamoto, the creator of Bitcoin, envisaged that it could prevent huge institutions from controlling the masses through their centralised systems.

It is not generally understood that when Bitcoin was launched over ten years ago, it was the Blockchain. It was the first technology that introduced the concept of peer-to peer transference of ownership that started with Bitcoin as money. Now, Bitcoin is becoming more well-known and used throughout the world but it is a threat to traditional methods of money transfer which is why the big banks are already doing everything in their power to confuse the public about its use and opportunities. They are using this time frame to develop and prepare their own version of the Blockchain to retain their power over the issuance of money. It will be just like the age of the car – they will want to place 'a man with a red flag' in front of it to slow it down so to speak. But will only slow it down for a while!

The range of its uses is truly mind boggling and outside the framework of most people's present understanding. For example, buying a house requires many professionals from different walks of life to become involved in the process; estate agents, lawyers, banks and financial advisers, all currently play their part and earn large fees from the process. Then, a whole series of procedures follow, involving the Land Registry, Local Authorities, amongst others before completion of the sale. The whole transaction can take months. With the use of what are called 'Smart Contracts' on the Blockchain, mathematical algorithms can be created that will ensure all the procedures are totally secure and take place in a matter of minutes, including the payment of the original contract, thus making the purchase of a house a ten-minute task before the keys to the new property are handed over. The same could apply to buying a car or anything else where third parties currently earn fees and commissions from people. This is going to mean many existing organisations losing their income earning capacity which will put them out of business.

Blockchain technology is predicted to change the way people come to understand issues of privacy and communication, as well as the convenience and speed of transactions that it will accommodate. This technology will affect the most basic reality of all – how we handle or understand money. It has the power to remove the power, currently held by the banks, and hand it to individuals, but it is still in its infancy in terms of recognition and the banks have enormous power and money to combat anything that they think might be a threat to their control over money transactions.

5G Mobile Technology – Caution!

5G is one of the latest technologies now being prepared across the whole of the US and Europe and is probably the most worrying of all. This is because there are clear intentions, certainly in the US, to avoid what is considered to be unnecessary regulation in order to ensure that the billions of earnings envisaged are not hampered by safety aspects that usually slows new innovation down. Most reviews state that 5G technology uses military grade software and that the infrastructure of thousands of antennas almost on every street corner will, according to many experts, actually 'fry' peoples brains. This may sound melodramatic but most research shows that these antennas will produce microwaves powerful enough to ensure that signals will not be lost going around corners, as happens with the current technology. A constant signal is vital for driverless cars, for example, because they must have to be able operate in safety. The irony is that it won't make much difference if the public choose to have a 5G phone or not, because it is the antennas that are the danger to everyone. Much research is advising extreme caution, which governments seem to be ignoring in favour of the tremendous growth opportunities and, therefore, boost in much needed taxation. The seriousness of the situation cannot be overestimated, but whether sufficient numbers of people will protest is yet to be seen. There are certainly many scientists and doctors who are reacting as can be seen from the reports sent to the United Nations below:

The current issue of the European Journal of Oncology contains a document dated 13th September 2017, the "International EMF Scientist Appeal" (EMFscientist.org) It reports that scientists have warned of potential serious health effects of 5G. It was sent to the United Nations and the World Health Authority and said;

"We the undersigned, more than 215 scientists and doctors from 40 countries, recommend a moratorium on the roll-out of the fifth generation, 5G, for telecommunication until potential hazards for human health and the environment have been fully investigated by scientists independent from industry. 5G will substantially increase exposure to radiofrequency electromagnetic fields (RF-EMF) on top of the 2G, 3G, 4G, Wi-Fi, etc. for telecommunications already in place for humans and the environment."

"We are scientists engaged in the study of biological and health effects of non-ionizing electromagnetic fields (EMF). Based upon peer-reviewed, published research, we have serious concerns regarding the ubiquitous and increasing exposure to EMF generated by electric and wireless devices. These include–but are not limited to– radiofrequency radiation (RFR) emitting devices, such as cellular and cordless phones and their base stations, Wi-Fi, broadcast antennas, smart meters, and baby monitors as well as electric devices and infra-structures used in the

105

delivery of electricity that generate extremely-low frequency electromagnetic field (ELF EMF)." https://www.researchgate.net/publication/298533689_Inte rnational_Appeal_Scientists_call_for_protection_from_no n-ionizing_electromagnetic_field_exposure [accessed Jul 09 2018].

Earth Now

But we are now seeing reports of an even greater potential threat to our privacy that demonstrates elites being able to maintain control over the masses. It is called *Earth Now.* This is a new company looking to provide satellite imagery and live video in virtually real-time. Its unsettling sales pitch describes a network of satellites that can see anywhere on the globe and provide live video with a latency of about a second. And a look at the start-ups' top investors gives a lot of confidence that this thing is happening. On Wednesday the 18th of April 2018, *EarthNow* announced that it will emerge from the so-called Intellectual Ventures ISF Incubator to become a full-scale commercial business. Its first round of investors is comprised of a small group of complementary powerhouses: Airbus, the Softbank Group, Bill Gates, and the Intellectual Venture Satellite-industry veteran Greg Wyler. The big question will be who will own and control such a gigantic system of surveillance?

Can we avoid being controlled?

I personally believe the answer is no because with such sophisticated and accurate satellite tracking as well RFID chips, DNA links in the body to the internet controlling the Internet of Things, the only thing that could prevent total control would be to accept a life without the internet. With all goods and services requiring internet as well as having access to money to pay for these things, it would not be possible to survive long

It is abundantly clear that the world has most certainly changed dramatically over the past ten years or so. We are now seeing and experiencing things happening in every walk of life that leave many of us literally out of breath just trying to keep up. Information and technology are changing on an exponential basis and the pace of life is getting progressively faster. It seems that not a night goes by without news reports of 'unprecedented' events taking place that eclipse the importance of yesterday's 'unprecedented' events. The planet seems to be having 'convulsions' as it tries to cope with major ecological, economic, political and technological changes all at the same time. It seems that events are clearly converging together and inter-connecting in so many ways as they lead towards a common end.

Chapter 6: Environmental Signs

It is clear that for many years now, the environment has become considerably more unstable. Reports about ecological disasters occurring throughout the world are reported almost daily in our news. These include earthquakes, fires, floods, droughts, volcanoes erupting and pollution of the skies, seas, lakes and rivers. It is openly acknowledged by leaders world-wide, that the number one threat to the very existence of mankind is climate change. It has been said for years that unless serious action is taken, the world is going to reach dangerous levels that will threaten all life on earth. World leaders have been regularly attending the United Nations Climate Change conferences over many years in an attempt to reach a joint understanding about how to solve the issues.

We are now being told by many so-called experts that over the next few decades there is only a brief window of opportunity left to minimize large-scale and potentially catastrophic climate change that, in their opinion, will extend longer than the entire history of human civilization thus far. It is said that policy decisions made during this window are likely to result in changes to Earth's climate system measured in millennia rather than human lifespans, with associated socioeconomic and ecological impacts that will exacerbate the risks and damages to society and ecosystems that are projected for the twenty-first century and propagate into the future for many thousands of years.

Environmental challenges do appear quite awesome and it is noticeable how the intensity of many of these incidents now causes the main stream media to report them as being

unprecedented. But there are also a significant number of incidents taking place across the world each day that are only reported by alternative media sources and by members of the public. There are many excellent You Tube channels which report on these things every day. It certainly appears that they are now happening in greater number and with a variety of extremes.

For example, at the same time that unprecedented floods are reported, there is also a growing awareness of massive water shortages occurring in major cities around the world. Many reports claim that these shortages may well become the reason for major wars. Pollution of the seas, lakes and rivers is reported consistently with regular pictures of sewage and plastics being dumped in the sea that cause the death of many sea creatures. There are also numerous reports about the number of mass animal deaths taking place on a scale never before experienced right across the globe, with millions being found dead in their natural habitat and millions of sea creatures washed up on the shores and beaches of countries throughout the world. The sheer number of creatures dying every single day is astounding and the statistics can be found on the following web site that deals daily with figures on a world-wide basis.

http://www.end-times-prophecy.org/animal-deaths-birds-fish-end-times.html

Then, there are other extreme examples, like the disappearance of insect life. I don't think I have seen more than a handful of insects throughout the summer for the past couple of years. In the Guardian newspaper dated the 17th of June 2018, science editor, Robin McKie writes 'Where are all our insects gone - there is a crisis in the countryside – and a massive decline in insect numbers which could have significant consequences for the environment and for mankind.' Similar reports can be found in numerous news reports and journals.

Many parts of the world have experienced extreme droughts for years whereas other countries have had unprecedented amounts of rainfall which has caused massive destruction. Millions of people in major towns are now experiencing huge forest fires devastating large areas of the countryside and destroying people's homes, some said to have been caused by acts of arson and others as a result of long term droughts. The destruction occurs on a massive scale and seems to be occurring in many different countries at the same time.

In the past, the public had to reply on the mainstream press for news, we now have hundreds, if not thousands of individuals taking pictures and video on their mobile devices of incidences in places that would never have normally received any coverage. Various web sites have been created over the years where individuals show this film footage and it is hard sometimes to understand why such extreme events are not reported on the main stream news. Such photos and film footage show the effects of extreme changes in weather and the huge amount of damage that is displacing and destroying the lives of millions of ordinary people.

Although most people seem to be unaware, there is much damage being caused by governmental attempts to change our skies in order to deal with the effects of so-called global warming. According to a report in the 'Independent' newspaper recently, *'95% of the earth's population are breathing dangerously high air pollution. The air quality crisis has gained greater recognition as the impact of air pollution has been better quantified. Total air pollution was responsible for 6.1 million deaths in 2016, with ambient (outdoor) air pollution being the largest contributor, accounting for 4.1 million deaths, according to a large-scale study by the Health Effects Institute. The problem is getting a lot worse as the Earth's population has rapidly urbanised. Global deaths linked to ambient air pollution are estimated to have increased by 19.5 per cent from 3.3 million in 1990.'*

For many years, the destruction of the air and the land has been taking place, affecting vast areas of forestation and vegetation throughout the World. However, such destruction is said to be no longer just due to climate change but also through man's attempts to rectify the situation through the use of Geo-Engineering. Most people have never ever heard of Geo-Engineering and yet it has been going on for well over 10/15 years in its current form. It attempts to lower the temperature of the sun by spraying a mixture of chemicals into the atmosphere. This has not only brought major problems to vegetation growth, but also to our personal health. Governments have managed to keep it all relatively secret by just denying that it even happens, despite all the evidence that is available to the contrary. I am not going to elaborate in more detail about this in my book because there are literally thousands of articles, books and documentaries that provide all the information anyone could possibly need. Perhaps the best source of information can be found on the web site www.geoengineeringwatch.com that has had nearly 30 million visitors to date if you want to learn more about how the planet is being purposely polluted by those attempting to 'save the world'. To become aware of all these things means making time to educate ourselves. This means, as always, re-prioritising our activities away from the constant sources of entertainment that we constantly indulge ourselves in.

There is obviously a great deal of data and information available to see the tremendous damage that is being done to the planet. We need to understand what the prophecies in the Bible have to say about these times because there is something much more important at stake.

Chapter 7: Rejection of Truth and Age of Deception

In this chapter, I consider what is happening in the church as the world moves towards the disruption that we can most certainly expect as a result of the unprecedented signs now taking place. I examine the implications for all those seeking to understand the times in which we now live as we move towards Jesus return. My understanding is fully based on the revelations the Lord has shown me and on experiences over the past 30 years since becoming a follower of Christ. All readers must, therefore, seek to verify whatever I might write with the scriptures and allow the Holy Spirit to bring a sense of truth.

The belief that Jesus Christ is the ONLY way to God is the most fundamental statement that in the eyes of a politically correct, 'Oneness' world, can only be regarded as a thoroughly intolerant and narrow view. This belief is, therefore, highly likely to produce serious implications for Christians including persecution and, in some circumstances, prosecutions. Legislation is coming into force throughout the western world that in effect denies the God of the Bible and is intolerant towards those who would proclaim or declare publicly that Jesus Christ is the *only* way to God. A challenge in this regard was brought when a member of the House of Lords asked the Government to confirm whether or not making the statement that Jesus Christ is the only way to God could result in prosecution. Needless to say, the Government spokesperson declined to answer. What we do know is that this declaration is most definitely not in line with post-modern society or 'spirit of the age' and will become increasingly unacceptable in the days ahead.

Throughout history, the particular spirit of the age, otherwise known as the Zeitgeist, has always prevailed and had its impact. If we are watching the signs of the times as Jesus expects us all to do, and have studied Bible prophecy, it should be apparent that the world is in the midst of a new Zeitgeist. Many people refer to it as the spirit of intolerance and rejection of objective truth. It is also referred to as 'political correctness', 'cultural authoritarianism' and 'identity politics', amongst others. This is the period in which the Bible speaks about the last of the last days. It is where the spirit of anti-Christ becomes all-pervading and eventually leads to the rise of the man described as the 'man of sin, or wickedness' i.e.

the final anti-Christ (meaning in place of Christ). He is prophesied throughout the scriptures and 'shadows' of his presence appear in the books of the Old and New Testaments. We are told that this anti-Christ will fulfil his purposes in accordance with the scriptures, first by bringing apparent hope to a world in turmoil, and then turning hope into a nightmare with an all-consuming evil agenda that leads to the eventual final encounter with Jesus: In 2 Thessalonians 2:8 it says:

"And then shall that Wicked be revealed, whom the Lord shall consume with the spirit of his mouth and shall destroy with the brightness of his coming".

When he comes into the public eye, this will be a time when, as the Bible prophesies; Satan will finally deceive millions of people from all religions into believing that he is the returning of Jesus Christ. Each religion is, in its own way, eagerly awaiting the return of their equivalent Messiah (Saviour).

Only One Real Saviour

The point is, that there is only going to be <u>one real saviour</u> and only spirit-filled Christians will know who he is. Everyone else from any other religion or faith, as well as nominal Christians, are going to have to decide if this presence is the real Christ or the anti-Christ. My question is, are we keeping watch and are we hearing what God is saying to us through the Holy Spirit, during these important days? One thing is clear, we are seeing this unique convergence of world changing events in the natural heightened by explanations taking place before our eyes in line with Bible Prophecy. Another, is that we are seeing destructive heresies being promoted all around us by those who have an interest in moving the world towards the acceptance of a One World religion that has no place for the fundamental doctrines of Christianity. What, therefore, are the major signs we see in the scriptures that speak of the impending return of Jesus? The most important is the rejection of the Christian message of truth and hope for the world (and this means rejection of Jesus Christ Himself), followed by an age of deception like no other in the history of the world.

What is Truth?

We are told in the Bible that when Jesus was being questioned by the Roman procurator Pontius Pilate, who subsequently had him crucified, he was asked directly, "What is truth?". As the scriptures say, Jesus remained silent and during this silence, Pilate probably concluded that Jesus was just a dreamer and posed no threat to the Roman Empire. But it was the religious Pharisees and Sadducees of the day who found him a threat to them; a threat to their power and prestige and to the very heart of their religion. That's the reason they wanted Jesus executed. Isn't it interesting to see how people can often hate the truth so much that they need to dispense with it!

It is said that 'those who do not learn from history are condemned to repeat it'. When we see globalist agendas, with their interpretation of truth and how we should all be 'thinking', we should realise that we are on the road

117

towards an authoritarian rule. This is most important, because most people and especially the young, seem to have so little interest in history. This may be something to do with the way in which it is taught, but it is the reason we are most likely to repeat the failings of the past. We now live in a 'bite sized' picture world, where everything is judged in a matter of seconds on social media including You Tube, Twitter and Facebook. It has become virtually impossible to determine truth from fiction and falsehood. The main stream media has become untrustworthy because it is incapable of reporting truth as the 'powers that be' are in total control of the content. This is now acknowledged by so many eminent people although most people simply don't realise the mainstream media is unreliable. But it requires the need to take our eyes off the mainstream media machine and tear ourselves away from the world of entertainment, designed to keep us all amused whilst world changing events happen without our even noticing. Failure to do so is also one of the main reasons why millions of Christians do not see the truth about what the Bible says will happen in the last days when an authoritarian world ruler rises to power. They simply do not spend the time reading it, let alone study what it says and relate it to everything that is happening all around us.

So, where can we find truth?

It can be found in the Bible that tells us Jesus Christ is God's only son. It is here in these scriptures that we hear Jesus tell us he is 'THE TRUTH'. The future has been set before everyone to see. So why don't we pay attention?

There are probably many reasons. Laziness, lack of time, lack of belief, or maybe because of sheer pride. Surely, we don't want ancient manuscripts to tell us how we should live our lives today! Do we really want to believe that there is a God who knows exactly who we are and what makes us tick?

'But Jesus did not commit Himself to them, because He knew all men, and had no need that anyone should testify of man, for He knew what was in man', (John 2:24-25), or Paul *'Now then it is no more I that do it, but sin that dwelleth in me. For I know that in me (that is, in my flesh,) dwelleth no good thing'* (Romans 7:17-19)

This is an amazing time to be alive in history but also, in many ways, a disturbing one. The reality unfolding before us presents us with the need to come face to face with the truth: to dare to accept that the Second Coming of Christ is a Biblical certainty that will bring this world as we know it to a conclusion. But first we must decide what we believe truth to be. The Bible tells us that *The Truth* is not a concept or an idea or a value system of some kind – it is a person. THE TRUTH IS JESUS CHRIST.

During his time on the earth Jesus moved amongst the people and answered many of their questions and he also made all sorts of statements and pronouncements. It is interesting to note how often he started a sentence by first saying "I tell you the truth." Over the years, many people have wondered why he kept answering in this way. My reply is always the same. Could it be that – he wanted people to know that before he spoke *he was telling us the truth?* He wasn't trying to deceive or lie to us or appear as someone he wasn't. The Bible says that he then followed this statement by teaching the people many profound truths. The most profound was that HE is the Way, the Truth and the Life and the *only* way to God. This is a fundamental starting point for anyone wanting to know what truth actually is: that Jesus Christ is God incarnate, God revealed to us in human form, our creator redeemer.

The need to consider the truth of this statement was proclaimed so clearly by the eminent Christian writer, apologist and theologian, C. S. Lewis in his book *Mere Christianity.* He said:

"I am trying here to prevent anyone saying the really foolish thing that people often say about Him: I'm ready to accept Jesus as a great moral teacher, but I don't accept his claim to be God. That is the one thing we must not say. A man who was merely a man and said the sort of things Jesus said would not be a great moral teacher. He would either be a lunatic — on the level with the man who says he is a poached egg — or else he would be the Devil of Hell. You must make your choice. Either this man was, and is, the Son of God, or else a madman or something worse. You can shut him up for a fool, you can spit at him and kill him as a demon or you can fall at his feet and call him Lord and God. But let us not come with any patronizing nonsense about his being a great human teacher. He has not left that open to us. He did not intend to."

Little else could be considered more profound than this. C.S. Lewis was giving us the only alternatives to understanding who Jesus was. He said that Jesus was either mad, bad or God. He didn't give us any other option and we are left to decide who Jesus is, which only we, as individuals can make. It is unavoidable, no-one can sit on the fence. The Bible tells us that if we are genuinely searching for truth, the Holy Spirit of God will reveal it to us., but we will all need discernment, because Jesus specifically warned us (Matthew 24) that in these last days we will be faced with deceiving prophets and teachers who will appear to speak much truth, but it will be mixed with a lie and God hates a mixture. This is what Jesus was teaching about in Matthew 13, with his parable around the introduction of 'leaven' or 'yeast' into the loaf. In scripture, leaven symbolizes the corrupting of God's truth by the introduction of evil, or false, doctrine. The big question we all face however is, can we see the small lie amongst the majority of truth? Are we receiving teaching that will enable us in this respect?

Is the Truth Easy to Hear?

If we are honest, the answer we would probably hear from most people is – probably not! But if we are to deal with reality, we need to hear truth, no matter how much it might make us uncomfortable or hurt. Hence the saying 'the truth always hurts'. But these days, so many people simply fail to examine the facts about any number of given so-called truths or situations. In today's mainstream media, we hear dozens of stories each day that cause us to react in various ways. And yet, how many people actually research the so-called facts behind such stories? People hold all kinds of 'beliefs', but how many of us stop to consider facts or evidence or to test the source from which they came?

As Christians, the beliefs that we may cherish should start with Scripture and our confidence should come from knowing the scriptures and our abilities to reason or debate from what is revealed in God's Word. How should we think about these things? Well, to start with we need to begin to study what the Word of God actually says and to discover how we can begin to determine the accuracy and the source from which scriptures came. If we are not going to be deceived, we also need to understand that the Bible is the revealed word of God and that it can only be interpreted through the help of spiritual revelation. When studying the Bible, we are meant to use 'exegesis' to extract what the Bible actually says, not 'eisegesis' where we read what we believe into the word of God. Today, we are surrounded by so many people teaching the word of God using the principles of 'eisegesis'. It is not just about having an intellectual ability as so many scholars simply believe. It is God's Word spoken to us. To maintain sound doctrine, we must be able to discern truth. However, hearing and acting upon the truth of God's word will bring persecution. Jesus clearly told us that *all* those who come after him and follow him, *will* be persecuted:

"And ye shall be hated of all men for my name's sake: but he that endureth to the end shall be saved. (Matthew 10:22)

"Yea, and all that will live godly in Christ Jesus shall suffer persecution." (2Timothy 3:12)

Truth Often Brings Persecution

The Bible clearly tells us that speaking the truth of the Christian gospel will bring persecution. Furthermore, it tells us that the world will hate followers of Christ for our beliefs, which include Biblical views about abortion, same sex marriage, gender identification, Islam, and the like. But this hatred is exactly what Jesus said would happen, especially in the last days before his return to earth. It is exactly what the Bible speaks about when it declares how the spirit of anti-Christ is now at work in the world in those who disobey God. Here are the verses in the book of Ephesians;

"As for you, you were dead in your transgressions and sins, in which you used to live when you followed the ways of this world and of the ruler of the kingdom of the air, the spirit who is now at work in those who are disobedient. All of us also lived among them at one time, gratifying the cravings of our flesh] and following its desires and thoughts. Like the rest, we were by nature deserving of wrath"(Ephesians 2:1-3)

In this remarkable passage, in verse 1, we see how God first spells out that we were all rebellious, and dead in what it calls *transgressions and sin* as we continued to gratify all our desires and lusts. It is referring to a spiritual death, not a physical one. So, what is it that continues to work today? It is the *spirit of the air* in verse 2. The word 'spirit', in Greek, is *pneuma,* which means in the breath or breeze of the air, so to speak. It is a kind of human attitude and way of thinking and acting. It is the spirit who is now at work in those who are disobedient (rebellious). This is the 'Zeitgeist' or 'Spirit of the Age' I have been speaking about. The Bible tells us that we are all obstinate and rebellious, with a totally fallen human nature, and lost without God until we come to the knowledge of the truth, Fortunately, God doesn't leave us without remedy for this 'god-forsaken' state of being, because when we come to recognise this fallen state in ourselves and choose to believe on the Lord Jesus Christ as our Lord and Saviour, we will find God's forgiveness and new life in Christ and be changed forever. We will have moved from darkness to light and our destiny will have changed forever.

Anyone who sees the reality of what is happening in the world should have a sense of sadness, because people are dying every day without the gift of salvation offered in Christ. Christians across the world are also dying horrible deaths each day because of their testimony for Jesus. But the Bible promises to all those who have received salvation in Jesus that a much better day is coming with Jesus' peace and righteousness reigning supreme over the entire world. In the meantime, what do we need to understand about this great time of change and what else could be affected? More importantly what does this all mean for the church?

Clearly, whilst being aware of the times, our focus must surely be on bringing others to the knowledge of the Saviour. It is vital that we show humility, but this doesn't mean compromising beliefs or telling someone they may be right when what they believe contradicts Scripture or even common sense. For me, it starts with recognizing that the source of truth is not in me. It starts with Jesus, my risen Saviour. He said, "I am the way, the truth, and the life," and he rose from the dead to prove that his words and his claims are true. Furthermore, that if he lives in me, I can see the truth in any given situation through the power of the Holy Spirit. The question is: Does he live in you and can you determine the difference between the truth and falsehood?

The Age of Deception

In the book of Matthew, Chapter 24, we see Jesus telling us the truth about the various earthly signs that will give advanced warning of his coming again. He mentions these signs once but he told us four times that we must ensure that we are not deceived by false Christs, false prophets and false teachers who will even perform miraculous signs and wonders. Jesus emphasises that the level of deception will be so great that even those who would consider themselves to be Christians could be deceived. This means we all need to consider how we currently discern good Biblical doctrine and truth from that which is false. So, **deception** is going to be the surest sign of the end times.

*"For there shall arise false Christs, and false prophets, and shall show great signs and wonders; insomuch that, if it were possible, **they shall deceive the very elect.**"*

In Mark 13:22 we read:

*"For false Christs and false prophets shall rise, and shall show signs and wonders, **to seduce, if it were possible, even the elect.**"*

In the book of Revelation chapter 13, verse 11-14 it says:

*'Then I saw a second beast, coming out of the earth. It had two horns like a lamb, but it spoke like a dragon. It exercised all the authority of the first beast on its behalf and made the earth and its inhabitants worship the first beast, whose fatal wound had been healed. And it performed great signs, even causing fire to come down from heaven to the earth in full view of the people. Because of the signs it was given power to perform on behalf of the first beast, **it deceived the inhabitants of the earth**'.*

These verses suggest that millions of people will be deceived and need to be warned about the sheer magnitude and utter power to deceive in this coming period. I believe that born-again, spirit-filled believers in Christ who are seeking to lead a holy life as they act in obedience to the Word of God and as they watch out for his return, will not be deceived. But the Revelation 13 scripture does speak of great signs and wonders that will include fire coming down from heaven. I wonder how many of us witnessing such a miracle would be able to decide whether this was from God or not? I wonder, without any preparation or teaching, how many Christians might believe that surely only the real Jesus Christ would be able to perform such a miracle? Maybe God is asking each of us whether we are 'the elect' in the first place?

Converging Signs and Rejection of Truth

Maybe, only born-again, spirit-filled Christians with the power of Christ within will be able to tell? Maybe it is a call from God for each one of us to check whether Jesus actually resides in us before this event occurs?

"Examine yourselves to see whether you are in the faith; test yourselves. Do you not realize that Christ Jesus is in you—unless, of course, you fail the test? (2 Corinthians 13:5)

Many believe that Christianity has now largely lost its influence in the Western world. It is now often said that the proof of this can be seen in the recognition of our having become, in the main, a godless society. There are, of course, churches across the Western world that proclaim God's supernatural power through the outworking of their ministries. Many of the mega-churches have been growing considerably in some countries, but the theology, or doctrine, behind some of these churches is not always working for good, and sometimes it is false. The need for spiritual discernment is as great as it has ever been and will be even greater in the days that lie ahead.

When preachers and teachers come to deliver what they call a life-changing ministry of the miraculous and healing, we still need to ask important doctrinal and practical questions if we are going to see the flock guarded by the shepherds. Unfortunately, it seems, that all too often, many unsuspecting and undiscerning Christians will chase after signs and wonders and can easily fail to pay attention to what the Bible calls sound doctrine. When asked to justify his ministry on one occasion through signs and wonders, Jesus said:

"A wicked and adulterous generation seeketh after a sign; and there shall no sign be given unto it, but the sign of the prophet Jonas. And he left them and departed." (Matthew 16:4)

After all, Jesus' most important warning was to 'watch out' for anyone who deceives and we have moved into serious deception in the church today, especially amongst many churches who previously maintained sound doctrine.

Compromising Truth in a Post-Modern Culture

We now see this 'spirit of the age' sweeping the Western world, that somehow imprints the need for 'equality' and diversity and inclusiveness on all it touches, almost at any cost. In fact, it produces a great deal of intolerance by those who say they are being tolerant and loving towards others. But more than this, it is causing division and hate, with laws being put in place to prevent anyone else from even having the freedom to disagree. We are in the age of what is called 'Post-Modernism'. This is a belief system. It is a faith of kinds, because its followers 'believe' that there is no such thing as absolute truth. To them, everything is relative; what you choose to believe as truth may not be what I believe. But that's apparently OK because as long as we all accept that everything is relative and as long as we respect each other, we can apparently hold our separate positions without any conflict. This is not only total nonsense; it is an outright lie, because anyone can prove scientifically and mathematically that there are absolutes and there always have been. If Professor Albert Einstein or Isaac Newton were still alive today, I am sure that they would have strong arguments against anyone disputing the respective Laws of Relativity or Gravitation and declaring that these scientific facts were only their own ideas of truth – none were absolutes! Try arguing that two plus two could, mathematically be anything other than four. These very people who say they are tolerant are often the most intolerant if you fail to agree with them. It seems to be producing a serious sense of division amongst people and causing a very 'mean spirit' to rise up and a very intransigent people who just have to be right despite the facts.

Can't we just have an 'acceptable' form of religion?

Whilst truth is being compromised, it is interesting to observe most 'worldly' leaders still believe in the need to maintain religion. This has always been seen as a means of bringing some sense of morality to society. The question is, what kind of religion and what kind of morality and what kind of truth? After all, it is becoming clear that it mustn't be one which includes absolutes, because we live in times when there is apparently no such thing, only truth according to individual interpretation.

The gospel of Jesus Christ, which is the power of salvation, is, therefore, going to come under severe attack in the coming days. Deception means that people are being persuaded to believe that the Bible and the scriptures have been misinterpreted or that they may well not even be true. As we continue to consider what Christians face in these days, we need to understand that we have reached a new stage in our modern Western world.

The Judeo-Christian heritage has previously been the bedrock of Western societies for centuries. Once this foundation is removed, it should not be a surprise to see most of the Western world, and certainly the United Kingdom, rapidly dissolve into a totally godless society. People need reminding that Christianity is actually based on pure *facts*, not on feelings or purely subjective views!

The question must, therefore, be posed: is the Christian Gospel still acceptable in our post-modern Western world where equality and identity politics have become the new 'religion' that seems to matter above everything else, where feelings trump facts? The signs indicate clearly that it is not. In this spirit of the age, there is the desire to prevent anyone the right to proclaim any absolutes that might detrimentally affect another person's viewpoint. It seems that people want absolute tolerance, just as long as our views are in agreement with theirs. It is, of course, acceptable for them to become intolerant with Christians. We now see that the only thing about 'acceptable religion' is that it must be non-threatening to anyone else's point of view which doesn't apply to the Christian faith. It seems that we must all simply learn to get along with everyone in the light of these newly declared norms. The reality is, however, that this is the beginning of the end of free speech and the path towards an authoritarian state and the One World religion that the Bible prophesies.

This is why the world will want another more acceptable gospel. It is why, in this current age, we are being introduced to a new thinking – a Christian gospel re-designed by something called the 'Emergent Church' phenomenon. It is important to understand that this is not just a rehash of the old New Age teaching from years ago, but a complete re-interpretation of the gospel, in line with the Zeitgeist 'spirit of the age'. This 'gospel' is being promoted by many previously highly respected evangelical leaders who are accommodating the 'spirit of the age'. But should we be surprised? After all, the scriptures clearly warn that a time will come when people will not put up with sound doctrine. In the 2 Timothy 4:1-4 the Apostle Paul is telling Timothy to:

"I charge thee therefore before God, and the Lord Jesus Christ, who shall judge the quick and the dead at his appearing and his kingdom; Preach the word; be instant in season, out of season; reprove, rebuke, exhort with all long suffering and doctrine. For the time will come when they will not endure sound doctrine; but after their own lusts shall they heap to themselves teachers, having itching ears; And they shall turn away their ears from the truth, and shall be turned unto fables.".

This scripture tells us clearly that people will no longer want to hear truth. They will instead want to hear anything that their 'itching ears want to hear' and truth will not be on the agenda. This tells us that the deception will be so great that even those who believe they are Christians are open to being deceived by the coming Anti-Christ 'replacement' for Jesus. The Bible says that the ramifications will be nothing short of horrendous, as the *'love of many will grow cold'* and people *'will hate one another'* (Matt 24) and even *'give one another up'* to the authorities.

Minority Rights Rule

The laws of the land in Western society have changed so rapidly that we have hardly had any time to think through why or how this pathway has been allowed to occur. After all, statistics seem to indicate that there are only minute numbers of people in 'minority groups' promoting minority positions like gay rights and gay marriage etc., and an even smaller number promoting neutralised gender laws. So how have we seen such radical and speedy changes that affect the whole of our society with the majority of people in disagreement? The ramifications are far reaching and indicate that it will soon become unacceptable to continue proclaiming the Gospel of Christ and to speak of sound Biblical doctrine as before. How long might it be before the Bible is actually banned?

If the Gospel of Christ, as recorded in the Bible, is to remain the foundation for a God-fearing society, it is surely concerning to see so many mainstream churches all too often accepting 'another gospel'. This 'other gospel' is one that consists of half-truths and the reinterpretation of scripture in line with the modern spirit of the age. What is really worrying about such a gospel is that it is really attractive because it doesn't challenge anyone about the destructive power of iniquity (sin). It appears full of love and grace and speaks about Jesus but says nothing about repentance and turning from the iniquity that indwells us that causes all our sins. It doesn't want to entertain traditional basic Christian doctrine about a God of judgement or wrath or about there being real places of heaven or hell. It is not about the real Jesus of the Bible, it is about 'another' Jesus. As a result, we are seeing so many Christians being swept up in the deception spreading across the Western churches. What is even more deeply concerning, is that it is often the very same churches that previously stood firm in preaching a gospel that condemned sin and upheld the need to be born again through the power of Holy Spirit, who brings a whole new life through Jesus Christ. The new gospel chooses instead to reinterpret the meaning of the words sin, heaven and hell, and even what it really means to be born again. It also changes the doctrine about the Holy Trinity and finally presents a more acceptable interpretation of the book of Revelation that excludes any such thing as God's judgement or wrath. This type of teaching is generally experienced through the 'Emergent Church' or 'Hyper Grace' movements. In reality, there is no unified and specific movement as such, but I believe there is collaboration between them. In truth, the Bible says we are in the midst of the period when there will be many more 'wolves in sheep's clothing'. It is clear that the 'spirit of the age' is most certainly amongst us, just as the Bible prophesies. There are, of course, severe consequences for teaching 'another gospel'. We read in the book of Galations, chapter 1 what the Apostle Paul said in verses 8-9

"But though we, or an angel from heaven, preach any other gospel unto you than that which we have preached unto you, let him be accursed. As we said before, so say I now again, if any man preach any other gospel unto you than that ye have received, let him be accursed".

So, for those teaching or preaching a false gospel, the Bible tells us clearly what God says: They should be 'Accursed'. It doesn't get much stronger than that! But there are other consequences as well for turning away from the truth of the Gospel of Christ and the truths about his crucifixion and resurrection. Total godlessness.

Godlessness in the Last days

"This know also, that in the last days perilous times shall come. For men shall be lovers of their own selves, covetous, boasters, proud, blasphemers, disobedient to parents, unthankful, unholy, Without natural affection, trucebreakers, false accusers, incontinent, fierce, despisers of those that are good, Traitors, heady, highminded, lovers of pleasures more than lovers of God; Having a form of godliness, but denying the power thereof: from such turn away." (2Timothy 3:1-5)

Many people will ask, where does all this intolerance and godlessness come from in the first place? When Adam and Eve rebelled against God as described in the book of Genesis in the Bible, the destiny for mankind was set in motion as they were deceived by the devil, or Satan, which means 'adversary'. The Bible describes this Satan as a powerful fallen angel who desires to be worshipped as God. His main characteristics are arrogance, pride and rebellion, and when man came under his rule, these same characteristics became seen in the heart of man thereafter. It birthed an inner desire of mankind to 'live my life, my way', without interference. This is the rebellion we see permeating our society, that starts in the heart and leads to a hate for God. William Barclay, the famous New Testament commentator, put it this way, *"But the sin of the man who is arrogant is in his heart. He might even seem to be humble; but in his secret heart there is contempt for everyone else. He nourishes an all-consuming, all-pervading pride; and in his heart there is a little altar where he bows down before himself."* Does not Barclay's definition of one who is arrogant capture what we are seeing today? It is not enough to have an opinion anymore, it has to be accompanied with spiteful contempt for all those who disagree. It is this pride that leads so many to ridicule opinions they disagree with. The ability to make a well-reasoned case to support one's point of view has degenerated into the art of personally destroying one's opponent. Arrogance breeds a sense that 'of course those who think differently from me cannot be right; therefore, I am justified in using whatever means necessary to destroy my opponent.' It's all about the politics of personal destruction at the expense of truth.

The apostle Paul used the word 'abusive'. This is what we witness more and more with insults towards God as well as other men and women. It is the verbal expression of contempt that begins in the heart of one who is arrogant that finds its expression in slandering the good name of others. In addition, we see that whenever anyone attempts to express a particular view, they are most often lambasted as being racist or a bigot, or that they must possess some dark and evil 'phobia'. Victories today are often measured in one's ability to convince the majority that one's opponent is racist, even if you must lie about what was said behind closed doors or twist words to make one's opponent appear to hate others. Paul also uses the word 'brutal' and 'lovers of themselves' to describe people living in the last days. In 2 Timothy 3, verse 3, the apostle depicts people during the last days as 'slanderous'. We live in a day where false accusations are the norm rather than the exception. The mainstream news is full of slanderous remarks made against all kinds of people.

The Bible says, forgive those who hate you and turn the other cheek. Love your enemies. This is quite different from the character assassination to silence a person who disagrees with you. Slandering people, ruining their reputation, calling them names, and getting them fired, is not of God. Clearly, we need to respect the opinions of others, even if we vehemently disagree with them, although it is sometimes difficult when those expressing these views get carried away whilst arguing their case. But we must remember that we can be confident of what we believe without impugning the intelligence of others. We are indeed living in the last days of human history and the dark days of the tribulation are rapidly approaching. What we see in our world is precisely what the Lord Jesus said would happen during this time, so it should not surprise us.

Giving One Another Up

Another important but very sobering sign of the end times is seen in Matthew 24:9-10 where Jesus said:

*"Then shall they deliver you up to be afflicted, and shall kill you: and ye shall be hated of all nations for my name's sake. And then **shall many be offended**, and shall betray one another, and shall hate one another. And many*

false prophets shall rise and shall deceive many. And because iniquity shall abound, the love of many shall wax cold. But he that shall endure unto the end, the same shall be saved.

In the King James version of the Bible, various words are used that are not well translated in all modern Bible versions. For example, in verse 10 the words are '**shall many be offended**'. This comes from the Greek word '*skandalizo*'. It means to entrap or, used figuratively, to trip up, stumble or entice to sin; apostasy. Today, we see so many instances of people being 'offended' by someone daring to have an opinion and then attacking them, often personally. People are being 'offended' when Christians declare the truth of the Gospel. Christians are even prosecuted if they dare to express a Biblical view about something. But this is understanding the word 'offended' within the context of the definition within our English language, which is 'to be resentful or annoyed, typically as a result of a perceived insult'. As I have stated above, the word '*skandalizo*' is much more forceful and purposeful than that. It means intentionally putting a stumbling block or impediment in the way, upon which another may trip up or fall and enticing another to sin or to fall away. The next word used in the passage is betray each other. The Greek word is '*paradidomi*' which means to deliver up, give over, recommend, put in prison, cast over, or commit. This is surely a difficult concept to come to terms with. It could mean members of our own family might give one another up to those in authority because of believing and declaring Christ is the only way to God. We, in the West, haven't generally experienced such a thing, but it is common in other parts of the world. It should not, therefore, come as a surprise because Jesus preached clearly that people will experience '*skandalizo*' by the use of his name and this will bring division.

One of the most famous films of all time that depicted this awful reality was *The Sound of Music*. Towards the end of

the film the Von Trapp family were attempting to escape the Nazis. Leisl von Trapp, the beautiful 16-year-old, and her family were hiding in a graveyard while the Nazis were searching for them. Her young

teenage lover was Rolf and they were both dancing arm in arm earlier in the film, very much in love. However, Rolf had now joined the Nazi party and was a part of the search. Peeking out from behind one of the graves, Leisl gasped when she saw it was Rolf and the sound alerted him just as he was leaving the scene. In a moment, Rolf had to make a decision; would he disclose the family's whereabouts, or keep quiet? Despite his love for her, he blew his whistle and gave them away. Nothing could be sadder, but this is what the Bible says will happen in these last days. Can we envision such a thing happening today? Quite possibly, when you see how Hitler was able to indoctrinate the youth in his day and as we watch the huge division that has been caused by various people groups taking a stance against each other in these days of political correctness and equality. But in the Bible, Jesus tells us that such division will take place as people decide between truth, deception and lies. He said clearly that he didn't come to bring peace on earth, but division.

"I am come to send fire on the earth; and what will I, if it be already kindled? But I have a baptism to be baptized with; and how am I straitened till it be accomplished! Suppose ye that I am come to give peace on earth? I tell you, Nay; but rather division: For from henceforth there shall be five in one house divided, three against two, and two against three. The father shall be divided against the son, and the son against the father; the mother against the daughter, and the daughter against the mother; the mother in law against her daughter in law, and the daughter in law against her mother in law." (Luke 12:49-53

Peace and Security and then Sudden Destruction

Jesus was telling us, plainly, that he knew the world would despise truth and that his message would cause division. The Bible says that Jesus knows that the heart of man is desperately wicked and selfish. (John 2:24). For if the world will actually despise truth in Christ and choose lies, it should not be surprising that it will search for a kind of peace that will suit its own desires. This is why the Bible states that in the end days, many will be crying out for peace and security but they will not find it. Instead, it tells us in the book of 1 Thessalonians that sudden destruction will come.

"For when they shall say, Peace and safety; then sudden destruction cometh upon them, as travail upon a woman with child; and they shall not escape, now brothers, about times and dates we do not need to write to you, for you know very well that the day of the Lord will come like a thief in the night". While people are saying, peace and safety; then sudden destruction will come upon them, as travail upon a woman with child; and they shall not escape." (1Thessalonians 3:5)

We are now looking into the face of major world conflict, including wars and rumours of wars building up in the Middle East which is, of course, the main focal point and key to understanding end times events before Jesus returns. The other major focal point concerns the amount of unprecedented world debt that continues to grow exponentially. It has now reached levels that are impossible to control and it is unrepayable, thereby strangling people's lives. This is why the future of the monetary system will play a very important part in these end times, because we are told in the Bible that it has everything to do with trade (Revelation 13:17). Trading with each other requires having access to money. Once the world's monetary system is in turmoil, and world 'fiat' paper currencies become unstable, the ability to buy and sell that people rely on for their continued existence and security, becomes threatened. This will lead to shortages in the basics of human life that enable people to sustain themselves. It will also lead to the value of investments, deposits and property being at risk of total loss. One only has to look back at the pictures of desperate people queuing outside the Northern Rock Bank in the UK back in 2008 when they were told that the bank had to cease trading. They stood for hours hoping to be able to withdraw their hard-earned savings when the banks began to collapse. This is just a tiny example showing how people are likely to react in the light of a much bigger and more extended crisis.

The world is in a very precarious position, standing at the edge of something no one has ever known before, with the intensity of world events gathering momentum. This makes it ripe for a period of massive disruption and it is exactly what will happen to fulfil the prophetic scriptures that speak of the rise to power of the anti-Christ, who will then present all the solutions needed to stem the crisis and thus cause people to believe in his ability to bring about peace and security. But the Bible says that when people say peace and security, sudden destruction will come.

One World Systems

As the world moves towards the end of the last days, the Bible once again shows quite clearly that world systems will operate on a centralised basis where all sovereign nations are brought to a common understanding of 'Oneness' under the control of the anti-Christ. In earlier chapters, I have described the part that money plays in our world and why is it so important to understand how it will have a significant role in the end times. The Book of Revelation clearly tells us that it is one of the most important signs to look out for because the anti-Christ will come to control the entire monetary system. It will be when he is able to demand that everyone receives a mark on either their right hand or their forehead in order to meet the requirements set by his authority. (Revelation 13:16) It is clear, that if we do not allow our bodies to be marked in this way, we shall not be able to sustain ourselves, because we will not have access to the monetary system. This tells us something about the direction in which our present monetary system will need to evolve. I explained this in the chapter on technology.

The Bible says we will also see the rise of a world

government system of some kind, through the bringing together of nations after the destruction of freedom and democracy. I believe that the 'Spirit of the Age', the Zeitgeist, will ensure the desire to make people believe that we can create a better and more fair and equitable Utopian world where everyone can live together in peace and harmony. This is, after all, the message being proclaimed by the far reaching United Nations Agenda 2030 now being brought into effect in most nations, backed by the Pope and numerous other groups. It is an agenda that is directly in line with new laws and regulations relating to equality, same sex marriage, the LGBTI movement, gender neutralisation etc. and is being branded as a new 'Vision' for the future.

Different gods!

Many people will ask, how could so many diverse religions with such different beliefs and different 'gods' ever come together to worship one god? As Bible believing Christians, it is because this is what the Bible prophesies will happen. In 2 Thessalonians we see that *all* people groups will end up worshipping the anti-Christ who declares himself to be god. It is an ongoing process that calls for unity and 'oneness' amongst different religions and religious leaders already taking place in order to deal with a world in turmoil and the desire for peace and security. This anti-Christ will seat himself in the holy temple in Jerusalem currently waiting to be rebuilt. (2 Thessalonians 2).

End Times Authoritarian Control

In order to achieve this final position of authoritarian control, as will be desired by the people, another major spiritual shift is necessary. This involves an amazing and strange phenomenon that has been growing right in front of our eyes for many years. It is what Professor Jordan Peterson has called 'Cultural Totalitarianism' or 'Identity

Converging Signs and Rejection of Truth

Politics', while Melanie Phillips calls it 'Cultural Colonisation'; others refer to it as the collapse of all moral framework. When law pronounces that there is no difference between man and woman, we should know that the nation has moved into a time of God's judgment. If we are Bible believing Christians, we understand that this is the basis of life and cannot be tampered with by man and his endless ideas. What makes it so much worse is the fact that there are only two biological sexes, and no matter what man might say to the contrary, everything else is a lie. But this is where, for numerous reasons, so many previously accepted normalities about human life have been challenged by a growing number of minority groups and their views forced into the mainstream.

However, it is clear that a total shift in the world's thinking will have occurred in order to establish the man called the anti-Christ into power and this will have to include the final rejection of absolute truth. More and more, we are becoming aware that it is less and less acceptable to be able to express an opinion or view that somehow disagrees with those who belong to these minority groups. But when the enforcement of minority views become enshrined in law, we are surely entering what can only be described as an authoritarian state. No matter how you may look at it, we are witnessing the silencing of opinion and free speech. This, in reality, is the final rejection of ABSOLUTE TRUTH! This is something we have never seen before on such a large scale across the Western World. Maybe Julian Huxley was accurate in his book *Brave New World* where he said people would finally invite this type of totalitarian view.

The Anti-Christ 'Saviour'

The arrival of the Anti-Christ into power will be greatly applauded by the world because of his apparent ability to offer solutions for all the world's problems. The scriptures say that this man will sign a final peace treaty with Israel and give the appearance of peace and safety. Clearly, it is most interesting that at this precise moment President Donald Trump is in the process of arranging such a peace treaty, having just acknowledged Jerusalem as the capital of Israel. This doesn't mean that he is or will turn out to be the Anti-Christ, but it does show that we could be drawing closer to the event. The US acceptance of Jerusalem as Israel's capital is, however, being seen by orthodox Jews as opening the way towards the rebuilding of the Jewish Third Temple and the re-establishment of the sacrifice according to many Jewish Rabbis. It is why we see a commemorative coin now being minted with the heads of King Cyrus and Trump, because of the sheer significance of this event. These are key prophetic signs that point to the nearness of the antichrist reigning from the Temple in Jerusalem. Whether this is the lead-up to this particular event or not, doesn't detract from the fact that the Bible tells us that it will happen at some stage and then, after a period of three and half years, the 'saving' anti-Christ demeanour will suddenly change as he reneges on his plans signed with Israel and he begins to introduce draconian laws that will not only plunge Israel into major problems but will prevent everyone from being able to buy and sell to each other without a specific 'mark' of his authority. The Bible says that for some, refusal to accept this mark will end in death but God is also a God of the supernatural and able to make provision for others.

And he had power to give life unto the image of the beast, that the image of the beast should both speak, and cause that as many as would not worship the image of the beast should be killed. And he causeth all, both small and great, rich and poor, free and bond, to receive a mark in their right hand, or in their foreheads: And that no man might buy or sell, save he that had the mark, or the name of the beast, or the number of his name. (Revelation 13:15-18)

God tells us clearly in the scriptures that anyone who takes this mark will forever be damned. Although this must sound very unpalatable, the scriptures explain why our own choices will eventually cause us to end up this way:

"And the third angel followed them, saying with a loud voice, If any man worship the beast and his image, and receive his mark in his forehead, or in his hand, The same shall drink of the wine of the wrath of God, which is poured out without mixture into the cup of his indignation; and he shall be tormented with fire and brimstone in the presence of the holy angels, and in the presence of the Lamb: And the smoke of their torment ascendeth up for ever and ever: and they have no rest day nor night, who worship the beast and his image, and

whosoever receiveth the mark of his name." (Rev. 14:9-11*)*

"And I saw thrones, and they sat upon them, and judgment was given unto them: and I saw the souls of them that were beheaded for the witness of Jesus, and for the word of God, and which had not worshipped the beast, neither his image, neither had received his mark upon their foreheads, or in their hands; and they lived and reigned with Christ a thousand years." (Rev. 20:4)

The nearness of this event is closer than at any other time in history. The technological advancement to enable such an occurrence is right here - now! To be taken along this abominable road, people must first be deluded into believing a lie; that all roads lead to God and that a One World Religion is what is needed to bring peace on earth. That the principle of 'equality' and goodwill to all men and a new properly controlled one world monetary system will bring stability. We must be led to believe the lie that the world's definition of 'equality' is the way in which, one day, everyone will be at peace with God. The aim is to get everyone to re-interpret the Bible differently; to get people to understand that a loving God, full of grace and mercy couldn't possibly be a God of wrath and judgement. To abandon all basic Christian doctrine and dispense with all the old-fashioned Biblical notions and distasteful beliefs; such as a God of wrath and judgement and eternal punishment. We must also apparently redefine what we mean by the terms heaven and hell and understand that Jesus never intended these to be literal places.

The Lateness of the Hour and Watchmen for Christ

It is an amazing thing to witness the revelations that God gave to myself and my wife 30 years ago, somehow coming into view in these days. However, it is only during the last ten years that I have been introduced to many other 'watchmen' whom God has called to sound the trumpet so to speak. The Bible says that

"When I say unto the wicked, Thou shalt surely die; and thou givest him not warning, nor speakest to warn the wicked from his wicked way, to save his life; the same wicked man shall die in his iniquity; but his blood will I require at thine hand. Yet if thou warn the wicked, and he turn not from his wickedness, nor from his wicked way, he shall die in his iniquity; but thou hast delivered thy soul. Again, When a righteous man doth turn from his righteousness, and commit iniquity, and I lay a stumbling-block before him, he shall die: because thou hast not given him warning, he shall die in his sin, and his righteousness which he hath done shall not be remembered; but his blood will I require at thine hand. Nevertheless if thou warn the righteous man, that the righteous sin not, and he doth not sin, he shall surely live,

because he is warned; also thou hast delivered thy soul.".
(Ezekiel 3:16-21).

Watchmen have therefore been put in place by the Lord to make proclamations just as John the Baptist did when Jesus first moved into the last three years of his ministry on earth. Watchmen are responsible for the lives of all those who would hear God's voice. This book is, therefore, my part in seeking to draw people's attention to what is currently happening throughout the world and to bring them to an awareness of the lateness of the hour. It is to warn them of the imminent return of Jesus Christ and to encourage them to understand what it means to be ready. My prayer is that this book will help everyone who reads it to realise the consequences of failing to be ready. After all, we are talking about an eternity set before us with or without God. What if today your soul is required by God and you were to die unprepared?

'But God said unto him, Thou fool, this night thy soul shall be required of thee: then whose shall those things be, which thou hast provided?' (Luke 12:20).

A sobering thought to be sure. But in the end, we must all take responsibility for our own spiritual well-being as well as praying for our families during this time, for who else will? May God bring you revelation and an awareness of his truth in these current times of serious deception, because now, more than ever before, Biblical truth is under serious spiritual attack and it will only be pure and absolute truth that determines the outcome and destiny for millions of people.

A World on the Edge
We are faced with making vitally important decisions. Are we going to be sold the concept of a Utopian world or  look at facts that declare reality? For those who do not wish to abide by Jesus' commands and who reject the Truth, the bad news is that we are not returning to 'normal'. Nor are we headed towards some kind of utopia as so many in the world and in many churches would have us believe. Despite all our efforts, we are not going to turn this world into such a place, despite thousands of Christians all working hard towards alleviating poverty or famine or war. We are not going to see the church arise to overcome the sin of the world as some evangelical leaders currently seem to proclaim. Does this mean we all stop what we are doing? No, of course not, because the Bible calls us all to be salt and light in a dying world.

"Ye are the salt of the earth: but if the salt have lost his savour, wherewith shall it be salted? it is thenceforth good for nothing, but to be cast out, and to be trodden under foot of men. (Matthew 5:13)

Chapter 8: Do we really want Jesus to Come Again?

If you consider yourself a disciple of Jesus Christ, then this chapter is for you. If you are not, I hope that you will still read it in order to gain greater insight into what Christians believe. All through the New Testament, Jesus told his disciples that they needed to be watching and waiting for his return. He told them very clearly how world events would unfold as we moved into the end times and that they needed to prepare. So, the big question is, if we are Jesus' disciples, are we preparing ourselves or just ambling through life thinking everything will go on as usual? If we are observers of the 'signs of the times' as Jesus commanded, it will be understood that we are now in the midst of numerous unprecedented world events. that are in line with prophecy written thousands of year ago in the Bible. Why did God give us this prophecy and why did Jesus tell us as much as he did about what would happen in the future. At the beginning of the book of Revelation, Jesus tells us that what is written therein is to bless us.

So, are you one of those who are watching and waiting, eager for Jesus' return just as he commanded? If not, and you are a Bible believing Christian, you might like to stop and take a good look at what the Bible says as well as looking at your own life and asking yourself a really important question: are you one who still finds hope in this world? Are you someone who would prefer to put the thoughts about this event out of your mind for just a while longer? If so, have you asked yourself what it is about your life that is so attractive that you would prefer Jesus Second Coming to be postponed for just a bit longer?

Maybe you have all sorts of plans and ideas about your future and maybe you are looking forward to any number of things already planned for your enjoyment. But the enjoyment of most things tends to be momentary. The excitement soon passes and we then start looking forward to the next thing. But not all people are able to enjoy our Western standards of living. The world is full of people who are suffering every day and would dearly love someone to give them a sense of hope for the future. Where can they find it?

Are Christians too much in love with the World?

It is interesting to observe that, despite the many unprecedented world-shaking events and persecution taking place all around us today, Western Christians still appear to be quite settled with their relatively comfortable lifestyle. Indeed, many do not seem to show any real signs of believing this world could be drawing to a close, let alone that Jesus will return just yet. But Jesus commanded all those who purport to follow him, to be keeping watch in order to prepare for his Second Coming. If you are still in love with the world and all it has to offer, you might find God's commands below to be rather challenging:

"Love not the world, neither the things that are in the world. If any man love the world, the love of the Father is not in him. For all that is in the world, the lust of the flesh, and the lust of the eyes, and the pride of life, is not of the Father, but is of the world. And the world passeth away, and the lust thereof: but he that doeth the will of God abideth for ever" (1John 2:15-17

But what are we keeping watch for?

Throughout the persecuted world, Christians are aware of how Satan is bringing destruction and death all around and they have a longing for Jesus' return. They long for the promises of God to come to fruition; they long for the redemption of their bodies and to be freed, once and for all from this life of sin. They long to experience the glory and the purposes that God has for all those who love Him and are called by His name. To live with God, their heavenly Father, face to face for all eternity. In the West, however, it seems so easy to become mesmerised into believing that the world is not such a bad place, and that we can change it for the better. In fact, much of the church these days seems to agree with this teaching that is often referred to as a post-millennial theology that results in something called 'Dominionism'. It places an emphasis on pushing back the powers of darkness and reaching every city for God with a view to presenting a successful church to Christ when he eventually comes.

Although many Christians probably accept that Jesus is coming someday – it seems that for many, it might be rather inconvenient just now! I am amazed at how many are able to convince themselves to believe that it probably will not be for a few hundred or even thousands of years yet, despite the prophetic scriptures that teach otherwise. Sadly, such a position is not often based on any solid theology. As a result of lazy theological exegesis, many leaders and believers conclude that we simply need get on with the job of living a Christian life the best as we can and try to transform the world – i.e. the theology of Dominionism. To those who hold this view, I would ask; what do you make of the scriptures containing prophecy that confirms the world will fall into greater and greater sin, leading to a time when Jesus returns a second time to wind up history, as we know it? Surely, the joy of looking forward, with great expectation, to Jesus Second Coming is because we know that we will finally be released from this body that is a slave to sin and that we will come into the presence of a loving Saviour. The events taking place, confirmed in the prophetic scriptures, inform us that we are now on the verge of entering into this whole new dimension of living. We are told that when Jesus comes, we will be changed in the twinkling of an eye and given new bodies designed for eternal life with Christ as King, with whom we will reign on the earth. What could be more exciting than this? What better hope can we have?

God is Revealing His Purposes

As we move closer to the end, it has become clearer, particularly over the past few years, that God is revealing his later day purposes to many more people. He is bringing revelation from the scriptures. At his first coming, Jesus said to the religious people of the day that they should have known when HE, the Messiah would come, because the time of His arrival had been prophesied for thousands of years before. So, why didn't they know who he was? Why didn't the Jewish leaders of the day, who knew the scriptures, know or understand the times that they were living in? This is all the more amazing when the Bible tells us that there were those who had been keeping watch and were able to interpret the times.

 Simeon, for example, who lived to see Jesus before he died – knew the times. His prayer that he might live long enough to see the coming of the prophesied Messiah before he died was answered. Simeon got to hold the Christ in his arms.

Then there were the three Kings who travelled a long distance to the place of Jesus birth, guided by God through the signs in the heavens – they knew the times. God says throughout the scriptures that we will see signs in the heavens that declare His glory. These Kings were and are, after all, part of the ancient old Christmas story. But God has told us there would be signs in the heavens to announce His Second Coming as well.

The Urgency of the Times

Today, God is once again enlightening many thousands of his followers who have also been keeping watch right across the globe about the current times and about the closeness of Jesus' return. I personally speak as one to whom God has laid on my heart the need to wake up from my own slumber and realise what time it is. I am not alone, for God has also introduced me to many others over the past few years who hear the same prophetic call. The word of God tells us in the book of Amos that God never does anything without first informing his people through His prophets.

"Surely the Sovereign Lord does nothing without revealing his plans to his servants the prophets" (Amos 3:7)

God is bringing a much greater sense of revelation in these days as well as an ability to see more clearly into the future through the scriptures. He is giving greater insight into the spiritual and the natural about the things that are to be, but only to those who are keeping watch and who have eyes to see. Therefore, before proceeding further, let me ask the following questions: do you have an interest in the future? Are you wondering what is currently happening in the world today or what will happen in the future? Are you keeping watch and do you desire Jesus' return with all of your heart? May God bring you revelation and an awareness of his truth in these current times of serious deception, because now, more than ever before, absolute truth is under serious spiritual attack and it will only be pure and absolute truth that determines the outcome and destiny for millions of people. The question is, will you choose to believe that there is such a thing as absolute truth? If you do, then you should find that *Jesus is Truth.*

Jesus said, "I am the Way, the Truth and the Life."
(John 14:6)

Because of a breakdown in trust, many people are rejecting all forms of authority. Never before have we seen such unrest sweeping the entire globe. We are headed towards a time when someone or something will need to rise up in order to bring a renewed sense of stability. Someone, whose authority will be unquestioned in order to bring about an answer to the current widespread distrust that now prevails amongst our political leaders. Most people in the Western world are now facing the most important question of all, "IS ANYONE THERE?" Is there anyone we can turn to in order to bring a sense of divine providence? Is it possible that a divine human presence could manifest itself in such a way that would satisfy all religions and nations and bring stability to our great unrest?

Shaking Foundations

Converging Signs and Rejection of Truth

As I have already said, this has been a thirty-year journey for me and my wife. From the moment of our joint acceptance of Christ as Lord of our lives and my wife's first dream about his Second Coming, to the present day when we see so many unprecedented events or 'signs' taking place around the globe that are confirmed in the Bible. Little did I realise that my career in banking and later, as an Independent Financial Adviser, all involved with the world of money would later bring about clarity as to how Satan will be able to gain absolute power over all nations and people groups when the anti-Christ is revealed, using the monetary system.

When I was just a couple of years into my research, God gave me another 'Word' in 2010. This particular 'Word' incorporated a sentence which said that he was *'about to shake the foundations of the earth and that people would curse His name'*. This occurred at the exact moment that I was questioning what I call 'world systems' and in particular the monetary system. I was having a kind of debate in my own mind about the implications that such controlled systems could have and coming to the conclusion that I could see our world monetary system literally crumbling before our eyes because of the lack of transparency and truth. I was praying in my own mind, having a conversation with God so to speak, asking Him what was happening as I saw the implications unfolding with greater intensity than I had ever seen before. The answer that He was *"about to shake the foundations of the earth"* resonated in my spirit as truth and I immediately knew it would have massive ramifications. But at the time I couldn't see what the phrase *"and the people will curse my name"* really meant or why He would say it.

Throughout the Old Testament, there are many references to God saying that He will shake the foundations of the earth. In the New Testament, in the book of Hebrews, Chapter 12:25-29 God says the words *"once more"* indicating the removing of what can be shaken - that is, created things - so that what cannot be shaken may remain:

"See that ye refuse not him that speaketh. For if they escaped not who refused him that spake on earth, much more shall not we escape, if we turn away from him that speaketh from heaven: Whose voice then shook the earth: but now he hath promised, saying, Yet once more I shake not the earth only, but also heaven. And this word, Yet once more, signifieth the removing of those things that are shaken, as of things that are made, that those things which cannot be shaken may remain. Wherefore we receiving a kingdom which cannot be moved, let us have grace, whereby we may serve God acceptably with reverence and godly fear: For our God is a consuming fire."

Converging Signs and Rejection of Truth

It wasn't until the last few years, as I studied the book of Revelation, that I could see more clearly what this 'shaking' meant. As with all things, I have found throughout my Christian life that God does not always give straightforward answers to our questions. It is as if He presents thoughts that resonate with us somehow in our inner spirit that leads us on the pathway toward a greater understanding about who He is and what He is really about. Here, we see God's final purposes revealed after everything that can be shaken, is shaken. But amazingly, it is here in the last few chapters that we also see people in the world actually cursing God to His face in their agony as He brings judgement upon the world as we read in the book of Revelation, Chapter 16, verses 9, 11, 21:

*"They were seared by the intense heat and they cursed the name of God, who had control over these plagues, **but they refused to repent** and glorify him. The fifth angel poured out his bowl on the throne of the beast, and its kingdom was plunged into darkness. People gnawed their tongues in agony **and cursed the God of heaven** because of their pains and their sores, **but they refused to repent of what they had done.** From the sky huge hailstones, each weighing about a hundred pounds, fell on people. **And they cursed God** on account of the plague of hail, because the plague was so terrible."*

The study of economic, political, technological and ecological events has shown clearly that the 'systems' of the world have indeed been going through a severe shaking that is growing in intensity and number. This is exactly what Jesus told us would happen when he used the words 'Birth Pains' to demonstrate that such things would happen with greater frequency and number just as what happens with child birth. Matthew Chapter 24:

*"As he sat upon the mount of Olives, the disciples came unto him privately, saying, Tell us, when shall these things be? and what shall be the sign of thy coming, and of the end of the world? And Jesus answered and said unto them, Take heed that no man deceive you. For many shall come in my name, saying, I am Christ; and shall deceive many. And ye shall hear of wars and rumours of wars: see that ye be not troubled: for all these things must come to pass, but the end is not yet. For nation shall rise against nation, and kingdom against kingdom: and there shall be famines, and pestilences, and earthquakes, in divers places. **All these are the beginning of sorrows.**

The Greek word for 'sorrows' is *'odin'* and this means *pangs, especially of childbirth: pain, sorrow travail.*

Recognising Jesus for who He is

Once we come to see who Jesus is, we have the opportunity to choose whether to believe there is such a thing as absolute truth or not. If we do, it is as if scales fall from our eyes and we are able to see clearly what is happening in the world and in the spiritual realms. We are then, as the Bible says, transferred from a state of darkness to light in the blink of an eye. Then as we continue to learn from the scriptures, we will see that a time is coming when Jesus will return once again to earth. The Bible says that at that time, we, the church, (*the Ecclesia or called out ones*) will hear the sound of a trumpet and the dead in Christ will rise, followed by those who are still alive to be caught up in the clouds to meet him in the air face to face as in the book of 1Thessalonians, Chapter 4, verses 16-18:

"For the Lord himself shall descend from heaven with a shout, with the voice of the archangel, and with the trump of God: and the dead in Christ shall rise first: Then we which are alive and remain shall be caught up together with them in the clouds, to meet the Lord in the air: and so shall we ever be with the Lord. Wherefore comfort one another with these words."

This was my wife's exact dream all those years ago. How amazing is that! As we move closer to the Lord's Coming again, both my wife and I are sensing a deep significance that the dreams and Words God gave us in our early years and the many signs taking place throughout the world, indicate that the time for Jesus' second coming is drawing near. It is my hope that Christians everywhere might have the courage to look through the illusions of life, into reality and recognise what has been developing before our very eyes for so many years. I hope that it will encourage everyone to look again into the scriptures and reconsider who they are in Christ, how and why they became Christians in the first place, and what their roles might be as we move closer to 'The Day'. But for now, we must also come to terms with another truth in the Bible. The fact that we will firstly move into times of severe tribulation, during which time our faith will be seriously tested. In fact, it is precisely because these times will become more and more intense that Jesus asked a very important question in Luke 18:8.

"Nevertheless, when the Son of Man comes, will He really find faith on the earth?"

Then in Matthew 24:10: Jesus says:

"At that time many will turn away from the faith and will betray and hate
each other."

The book Revelation means unveiling and this unveiling occurs more as we draw closer to Jesus' return. In this book, we can learn about God's full intentions for this world and the next. It is in these words of prophecy that **Jesus encourages us all to read, listen to and keep,** that we will hear what the Holy Spirit is saying to the church. At the beginning of the book Jesus says:

"The Revelation of Jesus Christ, which God gave unto him, to shew unto his servants things which must shortly come to pass; and he sent and signified it by his angel unto his servant John: Who bare record of the word of God, and of the testimony of Jesus Christ, and of all things that he saw. Blessed is he that readeth, and they that hear the words of this prophecy, and keep those

things which are written therein: for the time is at hand.
(Rev 1: 1-3).

I believe that we are witnessing the last stages of history before final onslaught of the spirit of anti-Christ and yet most Christians remain relatively oblivious to what is actually going on. Instead, we are watching many Christian leaders and teachers completely avoiding engaging with Biblical prophecy, with some even prepared to tell their congregations not to do so, because they believe that it will deflect people from their various outreach projects and good works. Some speak of the book of Revelation being too complicated for the average Christian person to understand, despite Jesus telling us we would be blessed by reading it. How can the last words of Jesus be too complicated for people to understand? Jesus clearly wanted us to know what lay ahead.

In the next chapter, I am going to do my best to set out my own understanding about the chronology of Biblical events. This is because I have found most Bible teachers to be rather confusing as they so often seem to teach what they want to believe rather than what the Bible says i.e. eisegesis instead of exegesis. I realise that in doing this, I open myself up to all sorts of criticism and opposition and many Bible scholars may hotly dispute my thoughts. However, this is something I am quite happy to risk, because I am merely stating what I believe the Bible says. If I am wrong, then I hope that the Holy Spirit will bring correction to me in the months and years ahead and lead you on the right road.

Chapter 9: The Day of the Lord

In this chapter, I want to look at what I believe the Bible teaches about 'The Day of the Lord', to see what can be expected as we draw closer to the Second Coming of Jesus Christ. This means trying to unpack a few things. I also want to try to outline the Chronology of events according to my understanding of the scriptures. You will need to do the same, seeking the enlightenment of the Holy Spirit.

The 'Day of the Lord' is often thought of as being a certain day, i.e. the actual day of the Second Coming of Christ. But it is not just about the moment that Jesus Christ appears. Most scholars agree that it is best understood as the period of human history when God brings about the final accountability for iniquity (sin). The study of end time events is known as the doctrine of Eschatology, but it is clear that over the past 40/50 years, this principle area of Christian doctrine has been sadly neglected. What has become apparent in these days, is that most Christians have received little, if any, teaching about the Second Coming of Jesus Christ or about the Day of the Lord. The question is why?

For centuries, the Bible has been taught in its entirety by scholarly, evangelical Christian teachers who have been true to the Word of God. I believe that a main reason that it is not now being accurately taught is because in these last days, the spirit of anti-Christ is preparing the world for what the Bible describes as the 'beast system' that will culminate with the arrival of a world authoritarian government, led by the anti-Christ himself in bodily form. At the same time that Satan is preparing the 'harlot' church, Jesus Christ is preparing the true church, described in the Bible as the 'Bride of Christ'.

However, before Jesus returns, he taught that there would be a great falling away from the Christian faith (Greek *Apostasia* – meaning revolt, defection). We are now witnessing such a falling away from truth into error and it is happening before our eyes in many mainstream churches, as well as evangelical churches, led by leaders previously highly regarded as preachers of truth. The Christian faith, based on the Word of God, has come under severe attack and is being reinterpreted in line with the current zeitgeist (spirit of the age), as well as being questioned as the basis for absolute truth. The Bible tells us that in the end times, Christian doctrine will be replaced by doctrines of demons that declare there is no such thing as absolute truth.

Converging Signs and Rejection of Truth

'Now the Spirit speaketh expressly, that in the latter times some shall depart from the faith, giving heed to seducing spirits, and doctrines of devils.' (1Timothy 4:1)

Studying the Scriptures - Exegesis vs Eisegesis

One of the main reasons for confusion in interpreting the Bible is because people insist on reading into the scriptures their own preconceived ideas. In studying the Bible, I believe it is really important to consider the meaning of words from the original text using the principle of exegesis (extracting what the scriptures say) as opposed to eisegesis (reading into the scriptures preconceived views). All Christians are responsible to feed themselves from the Word of God, asking the Holy Spirit to reveal truth. So, why is it that so many believe so many different things? Clearly, lack of sound Biblical teaching is the main cause. It seems that so many Christians just do not accept any of these events will occur during their lifetimes, although they could not explain why they think this. But many simply do not seem to have the desire to even find out, especially if they are enjoying this world and all it has to offer. As I say, I can only explain such chronology from my own study and understanding of the scriptures, which is of course influenced by Bible scholars. But it is also influenced by the continual prompting of the Holy Spirit and the dreams that my wife had at the beginning of our Christian lives which I covered earlier. In considering the chronology of the end time events there some really important questions to consider.

Converging Signs and Rejection of Truth

Jesus said that the world would suffer a period of great tribulation before his return, but would this be before or after the removal of the true church from the face of the earth in what Christians call the rapture? The Bible says that the world will suffer from the Wrath of God, but will Christians be on the earth to experience it, and what is meant by the Wrath of God anyway? The Bible teaches that Christ will reign on the earth for a thousand-years (The Millennium) together with his true and faithful followers; will this be literal or figurative? The Bible teaches that a time is coming when God will judge everyone who has ever lived in what it describes as the Great White Throne Judgment. What will be the outcome? Finally, the Bible says that God will make everything new; a brand-new heaven and a brand-new earth, which only those declared by God to be his true children, will inhabit. What happens to everyone else? Such important questions. I wonder how many people know what the Bible says? Surely, every Christian would want to know? If that is you, then can I urge you to read your Bible straight away to see what God has in store. Seek out sound expository Bible teachers and study the prophetic scriptures for yourselves, asking the Holy Spirit to bring you into all truth. I mention some of the most important in my final chapter. Because it is not within the remit of this book to answer all these questions, I am going to try and bring clarity to those I believe are the most controversial.

The Day of The Lord

Converging Signs and Rejection of Truth

The physical Second Coming of Jesus, will be beyond our human experience. To witness Jesus, appear in the clouds in power and great glory will be beyond anything we could imagine:

"And then shall appear the sign of the Son of man in heaven: and then shall all the tribes of the earth mourn, and they shall see the Son of man coming in the clouds of heaven with power and great glory." (Matthew 24:30)

How mind boggling to think that the whole world will be able to see him at the same time, but how astonishing to think that 'all the tribes of the earth will mourn'. How is that possible on such a joyous occasion? Most Bible commentators agree that Jesus was reminding all those who rejected Christ during their lives, including the Jews who do not accept Jesus as their Messiah, that they would mourn. This is because, the Jews will finally come to see with their own eyes that Jesus always was and is their Messiah – the Saviour of mankind and the one they have been waiting for. All the Gentiles (everyone else on earth) will also suddenly realise that he is God and yet they too rejected God's offer of salvation through Christ's sacrifice on the cross. Their religious beliefs, pride, obstinacy or satisfaction with this world and all it has to offer has led to this final point, when it is too late for repentance. The world will have reached the end of the church age of grace. It is the point at which the rapture occurs; the removal of the faithful church (the *Harpazo*) and the commencement of the next dispensation or era.

Converging Signs and Rejection of Truth

The Lord is not willing that any should Perish

But this 'Day' will not come without God having first exercised great mercy and patience, with the promise that he would not close down history until the very last person is gathered:

The Lord is not slack concerning His promise, as some men count slackness, but is longsuffering toward us, not willing that any should perish, but that all should come to repentance. (2 Peter 3:9)

The Bible tells us however, that when the time of mercy and patience is over, God's focus will return, once again, to Israel, when he will fulfil all the promises in the scriptures regarding his own people, the Jews. It will be when he begins to release his Wrath towards all those who loved darkness rather than light; all those who rejected the offer of his one and only Son, Jesus Christ and who wanted to have nothing to do with God. Nothing could be sadder than to realise, in an instant, that it is too late to decide for Christ. To reach a point when you know that, throughout your life on earth, although you heard the truth of the gospel, you chose to reject the offer. In the Gospels of Matthew, Mark and Luke we find Jesus speaking to his disciples and the multitudes who had gathered to listen to him. He was reminding them why he had come to earth and he called them hypocrites for not being able to discern the signs of the times of his first coming. He reminded them that the scriptures had not only provided a clear indication of when that would be, but they also provide a clear indication when he will come a second time and what will follow.

Let's look at the events in more detail.

Taking a Final Stand

Before we look, let us remember that in all this, Paul continues in his Epistle to the Thessalonian church to thank God for those loved by God and chosen to be saved through the sanctifying work of the Spirit and through belief in the truth. He says, stand firm and hold on to the teachings they had received. He prayed that God our Father would, by his grace, give courage and strengthen them in every good deed and word during this time. He reminded the Christians that God would strengthen and protect them from the evil one. (2 Thessalonians 2: 13-17).

In the coming build-up towards the great tribulation that Jesus warns about in Matthew 24, now spreading throughout the Western nations, it is clear that Christians are going to need to take a stand just as they do in heavily persecuted nations. Whilst it has always been necessary to put on the full armour of God (Ephesians 6:10-18) to stand firm against the evil one, this will be a time when it will become an imperative. Without this armour, no-one will be able to stand firm in Christ. For this is the time that the 'anti-Christ spirit' of which I have been speaking, will bring a form of oppression never before experienced. This has been developing momentum for the past 60 years or so and is now manifesting itself in the greatest culture war ever known as we head towards the events clearly prophesied in the Bible. It is in the Gospels that Jesus speaks clearly about the times in which we now find ourselves, and in the Epistles, where the Apostle Paul does the same. They both identified the pathway that the anti-Christ spirit will follow.

The Great Tribulation

In the Bible, (Matthew 24, Mark 13 and Luke 21), Jesus Christ first describes all the signs or events that will take place before his return. We outlined these in the first few chapters. He says that the earth will experience a time of trouble (Greek *thlipsis* = times of troubles = tribulation) unlike any previously experienced in the history of the world and never to be experienced again. We are witnessing a build-up of persecution of Christians that is becoming more pronounced throughout the Western world. As I have previously stated, the word tribulation *(thlipsis)* means, suffering distress, affliction, to hem someone in, to feel constricted, the feeling that there is no way to escape. Of course, there has always been tribulation but not like the tribulation that Jesus now describes, because he says it will be worse than anything the world has ever experienced. In Matthew 24 he says it will a time of GREAT Tribulation.

Into this time of great tribulation, the Bible tells us, the anti-Christ will come to the fore. In the book of 2 Thessalonians 2, we learn that he will take a position of power in the temple in Jerusalem (now being prepared). He will declare himself to be God and receive worship as God by all people groups.

'Who opposeth and exalteth himself above all that is called God, or that is worshipped; so that he as God sitteth in the temple of God, shewing himself that he is God.'

He will deceive people into this belief by performing miracles and signs, including calling fire down from heaven, in the full view of men (Revelation 13:13). During this terrible time on the earth we are told that he will deceive all those who are perishing with every sort of evil, and God tells us they perish because they refuse to love the truth and so be saved. We are then told that for this reason, God sends a powerful delusion so that they will believe the lie and so be condemned as they have not believed the truth but have delighted in wickedness. (2 Thessalonians 2: 9-12). In Matthew 24: 21-22 we read that this period of tribulation would need to be cut short, in order to prevent all mankind from perishing under such authoritarian rule. It will be cut short by an event called the rapture as Jesus comes in the clouds:

"For then shall be great tribulation, such as was not since the beginning of the world to this time, no, nor ever shall be. And except those days should be shortened, there

175

should no flesh be saved: but for the elect's sake those days shall be shortened.

The Second Coming of Christ and the Rapture *(Harpazo)*

Jesus coming in the clouds is what follows this period of tribulation. It is the Second Coming of Christ in all his glory. The Bible then says all true believers and followers of Christ will be raptured. There is no such word as rapture in the Bible. The term comes from the Greek the word *harpazo* which means, to be snatched away, as if by force. Jesus will literally snatch his faithful followers from the face of the earth in the blink of an eye as he comes again. At that moment, with the sun darkened and the moon no longer giving light and with stars falling from the heaven and with all faithful Christians (the elect) having been 'snatched' *(harpazo),* gathered, removed, from the earth by God, Jesus will appear.

'Immediately after the tribulation of those days shall the sun be darkened, and the moon shall not give her light, and the stars shall fall from heaven, and the powers of the heavens shall be shaken: And then shall appear the sign of the Son of man in heaven: and then shall all the tribes of the earth mourn, and they shall see the Son of man coming in the clouds of heaven with power and great glory. And he shall send his angels with a great sound of a trumpet, and they shall gather together his elect from the four winds, from one end of heaven to the other.' (Matthew 24: 29-31)

Converging Signs and Rejection of Truth

'Behold, he cometh with clouds; and every eye shall see him, and they also which pierced him: and all kindreds of the earth shall wail because of him. Even so, Amen.' (Revelation 1:7)

'And then shall they see the Son of man coming in the clouds with great power and glory.' (Mark 13:26)

As the true believers lose gravity, they will rise to meet Jesus in the air, exactly in line with the dream that God gave my wife at the beginning of our new life in Christ 30 years ago.

'Then we which are alive and remain shall be caught up together with them in the clouds, to meet the Lord in the air: and so shall we ever be with the Lord.' (1 Thessalonians 4:17)

The age of the church, also known as the age of grace, will have ended, thereby cutting short any further involvement of Christians with the Anti-Christ rule. God will have removed them from what is next to come:

'And except those days should be shortened, there should no flesh be saved: but for the elect's sake those days shall be shortened.' (Matthew 24:22, Mark 13:20).

It is important to understand that many Bible teachers refer to the Rapture taking place completely unexpectedly as a 'thief in the night'. I therefore believe it is important to challenge the most commonly held belief about a secret

177

rapture of the church occurring *before* any tribulation (known by Christians as the 'pre-trib rapture' position) takes place. There is nothing in the Bible that justifies this position or view, other than using the principle of *eisegesis* to impose your own view on the scriptures. In 1 Thessalonians, Paul was addressing the Christians who were worried that they had somehow missed Jesus return and not been 'raptured'. Let's give a little further thought to what the Bible teaches about the concept of 'the thief in the night' secret rapture that Jesus can come at any time and at any moment without warning.

Matthew 25:13 —*"Watch therefore, for you know neither the day nor the hour in which the Son of Man is coming."*

Mark 13:32-35 —*"But of that day and hour no one knows, not even the angels in heaven, nor the Son, but only the Father. Take heed, watch and pray; for you do not know when the time is. It is like a man going to a far country, who left his house and gave authority to his servants, and to each his work, and commanded the doorkeeper to watch. Watch therefore, for you do not know when the master of the house is coming—in the evening, at midnight, at the crowing of the rooster, or in the morning—"*

Luke 21:34-35 —*"But take heed to yourselves, lest your hearts be weighed down with carousing, drunkenness, and cares of this life, and that Day come on you unexpectedly. For it will come as a snare on all those who dwell on the face of the whole earth."*

Converging Signs and Rejection of Truth

Luke 12:35-40 —*"Let your waist be girded and your lamps burning; and you yourselves be like men who wait for their master, when he will return from the wedding, that when he comes and knocks they may open to him immediately. Blessed are those servants whom the master, when he comes, will find watching. Assuredly, I say to you that he will gird himself and have them sit down to eat, and will come and serve them. And if he should come in the second watch, or come in the third watch, and find them so, blessed are those servants. But know this, that if the master of the house had known what hour the thief would come, he would have watched and not allowed his house to be broken into. Therefore, you also be ready, for the Son of Man is coming at an hour you do not expect."*

2 Peter 3:10 —*"But the day of the Lord will come as a thief in the night, in which the heavens will pass away with a great noise, and the elements will melt with fervent heat; both the earth and the works that are in it will be burned up."*

Revelation 3:3 —*"Remember therefore how you have received and heard; hold fast and repent. Therefore, if you will not watch, I will come upon you as a thief, and you will not know what hour I will come upon you."*

Revelation 16:15 — *"Behold, I am coming as a thief. Blessed is he who watches, and keeps his garments, lest he walk naked and they see his shame."*

Are you keeping Watch?

The first point to understand, is that Jesus told us to keep watch. But what are we to keep watching for if we will be given no warning about when he will come? The second point is that the scriptures tell us that we will not know the DAY or the HOUR, but they do not say that we will not know the season. Jesus said, blessed are those who he finds WATCHING when he comes. Jesus will only be a thief to Christians IF we are not keeping watch.

Let's look some more. In each of these scriptures, the Bible says that Jesus will come at an hour or day when he is not expected. Clearly, we will not know whether it be in the morning, the evening or in the middle of the night, although this is the most likely time according to the scriptures. We can conclude that whilst this is true for all those who have no faith in Christ and for those who have rejected the Christian gospel, it is not true for Christians who have remained obedient to Christ and who have been keeping watch in accordance with Jesus commands. Why do I say this? Because Jesus warned that we should know the seasons of his coming from the prophetic scriptures and in 1 Thessalonians 5:2-6 we read;

*"For you yourselves know perfectly that the day of the Lord so comes as a thief in the night. For when **they** say, "Peace and safety!" then **sudden destruction comes upon them**, as labour pains upon a pregnant woman. And **they** shall not escape. But you, brethren, are not in darkness, so that this Day should overtake you as a thief. You are all sons of light and sons of the day. We are not of the night nor of darkness. Therefore, let us not sleep, as others do, but let us watch and be sober.* (Emphasis mine)

180

In these verses, the apostle Paul was speaking to the Christians. When he refers to 'THEY' or 'PEOPLE' saying peace and safety, it seems clear he is talking about everyone else apart from Christians. He tells them that sudden destruction comes upon THEM, that THEY will not escape sudden destruction. He explains that he doesn't need to teach the Christians in the church of Thessonalica about this event because **they would not be surprised.** Christians are not going to experience 'sudden destruction'.

"But *"you brothers are not in darkness so that this day should surprise you like a thief."* For when **they** say, *"Peace and safety!"* then **sudden destruction comes upon them**, as labour pains upon a pregnant woman. **And they** shall not escape. " (Emphasis mine)

So, it is when 'THEY' are saying peace and safety that sudden destruction comes and they will not escape. The point is, that Christians are escaping God's Wrath because they will know the times and the seasons as foretold in the scriptures and by the signs, but **They** (i.e. non-Christians) will not recognise the times or the seasons.

It is therefore clear that true followers of Christ will still be around during the period of tribulation, although they do not know the point at which they are going to be removed (*Harpazo*) from the earth. In my opinion, this makes the view, that Christians will not suffer any tribulation before Jesus comes, also known as the Pre-Tribulation rapture, unbiblical. This view was introduced in the early 1800s but it was not held by any the early church fathers. It is only in recent years that this teaching has begun to be heard.

The Wrath of God

Jesus said that IMMEDIATELY AFTER the Great Tribulation, He would come and this would trigger the release of the Wrath of God upon the earth. However, in accordance with the scriptures, Christians (the faithful church) will have been removed in the *harpazo* and they will not, therefore, suffer the Wrath (Greek *orgé*) of God. Why? Because the Bible says that the 'elect' (those who born again through the Spirit of God) are not destined to do so.

'For God has not destined us for wrath, but to obtain salvation through our Lord Jesus Christ, who died for us so that whether we are awake or asleep we might live with him.' (1 Thessalonians 5:9-10)

To gain a full understanding, we need to consider what the Greek word for wrath *orgé* means. It is used whenever the word wrath is used in the Bible throughout the New Testament. It comes from the word *orgáō*, meaning to 'to teem, to swell'; and thus, implies that it is not a sudden outburst, but rather (referring to God's) fixed, controlled, violent passionate feeling against sin, a settled indignation, justifiable abhorrence; by implication punishment, anger, vengeance, wrath. The Bible says in the book of Romans, Chapter 1: 18-32, that at one time we were all children of God's wrath (*orgé*)', but that was

182

because of our fallen rebellious nature. This wrath was removed the moment we accepted Jesus by faith as our Saviour. In the book of Ephesians 2: 1-5 we read that we are all affected and controlled by 'Iniquity' (Sin) which is the disease mankind comes into the world carrying at birth and it can only be dealt with by coming to accept the one who came to pay the price for this condition. It was through the death and resurrection of the Lord Jesus Christ as our Saviour and Redeemer. He paid the price for this condition and sets us free when we come to believe in him.

'And you hath he quickened, who were dead in trespasses and sins; Wherein in time past ye walked according to the course of this world, according to the prince of the power of the air, the spirit that now worketh in the children of disobedience: Among whom also we all had our conversation in times past in the lusts of our flesh, fulfilling the desires of the flesh and of the mind; and were by nature the children of wrath, even as others. But God, who is rich in mercy, for his great love wherewith he loved us, Even when we were dead in sins, hath quickened us together with Christ, by grace ye are saved".

So, it is by grace (the undeserved favour of God), that we receive this great salvation (by faith and faith alone). It is then that we become born-again believers in Christ. We receive a new spirit and we know that we are God's children. We are forgiven for all the sins we may have committed and we are saved from God's coming wrath.

Are we amongst the 'Scoffers'?

In 2 Peter 3: 3-13 we read that although true believers will be watching and waiting for the return of the Lord, there will be people who scoff at the idea because of their refusal to believe the truth of Jesus and their desire to follow their own ways:

"Knowing this first, that there shall come in the last days scoffers, walking after their own lusts, And saying, Where is the promise of his coming? for since the fathers fell asleep, all things continue as they were from the beginning of the creation. For this they willingly are ignorant of, that by the word of God the heavens were of old, and the earth standing out of the water and in the water: Whereby the world that then was, being overflowed with water, perished: But the heavens and the earth, which are now, by the same word are kept in store, reserved unto fire against the day of judgment and perdition of ungodly men. But, beloved, be not ignorant of this one thing, that one day is with the Lord as a thousand years, and a thousand years as one day. The Lord is not slack concerning his promise, as some men count slackness; but is longsuffering to us-ward, not willing that any should perish, but that all should come to repentance. But the day of the Lord will come as a thief in the night; in the which the heavens shall pass away with a great noise, and the elements shall melt with fervent heat, the earth also and the works that are therein shall be burned up. Seeing then that all these things shall be dissolved, what manner of persons ought ye to be in all holy conversation and godliness, Looking for and hasting unto

the coming of the day of God, wherein the heavens being on fire shall be dissolved, and the elements shall melt with fervent heat? Nevertheless we, according to his promise, look for new heavens and a new earth, wherein dwelleth righteousness". (2 Peter 3)

The scriptures make it clear that when Jesus comes again, everyone on earth will have had the chance of responding to the gospel, because he said that God would not close down this point in history until the whole world had heard the truth. There is no excuse and they know it. The Bible makes it clear how God loves his creation and wants to ensure that the very last person on earth is brought to the knowledge of salvation. But it shows how resistant some people will be until the very end. This is the spiritual war that the Bible describes all the way through and the reason we struggle in this life and become entangled in sin.

Before moving on, may I, once again, urge you to study a reliable Bible that includes original text, to determine for yourself all these 'Day of the Lord' events and their Chronology. It will mean seeking out all the prophetic scriptures from both the Old and the New Testaments, some of which I mention in my last chapter. The events that follow the completion of the Wrath of God are truly inspiring as we see what God has in store for all those who love Him and are called according to His good purposes in Christ.

Converging Signs and Rejection of Truth

In the next chapter I want to remind readers what is meant by the great spiritual battle in which we are all involved until Jesus comes again.

Chapter 10: The Great Spiritual Battle

Before we move on to the next chapter, I would like us to take a few minutes to consider this great spiritual battle that I have been referring to so far. Some readers might still find it difficult to believe that God really exists. I find it very interesting, when people find themselves in life threatening difficulties. It is only then, that they so often pray, even if they don't believe God exists. People even plead with God and make promises to give their lives to him, IF he will only save them from the situation in which they find themselves.

Is Anyone There?

As we go through the ups and downs of life and continue to be subjected to the 'troubles' of this world, there are moments when most people wonder if there is a God at all. Unfortunately, when things are all going well, we don't even think about God but when we get into deep

Converging Signs and Rejection of Truth

trouble and panic and don't know what else to do, we can easily find, at the last minute, the need to call out to God - are you there? Are you real? If so, can you help me at this moment when all else is failing?

This reminds me of the following joke. One day, a man was walking along the edge of a cliff on a lovey day, just taking in the sun when suddenly his foot slips and he tumbles over the edge. His heart skips a beat as he thinks he will fall and die but he just about manages to save himself by grabbing hold of a protruding branch that stops his fall. He looks down and his heart skips another beat as he realises the fall is steep and would mean certain death on the rocks below. He stops for a moment and shouts out, softy at first, because his heart beats so fast, "Is there anyone there?" No answer. He manages to shout out again, only a little louder, "Help, is there anyone there?" After a minute of agonising silence, an answer comes: "Yes, my son, I am here." The man jumps for joy in his heart as he realises he might be saved from certain death. The voice speaks again, "Just let go of the branch and I will catch you in my arms." The man looks down at the waves crashing against the rocks and sees that there is no-one there. He waits a minute and then finally shouts out "Is there anyone else there?" This is the same for many people. At the exact moment God could have stepped in to our lives, we lacked faith that he really existed because to do so meant taking action. In the story, the man had to let go and trust in this voice he was hearing but not seeing. This required faith.

Converging Signs and Rejection of Truth

The Bible gives us a clear picture of the story of life but, as a Christian, it is all about a life of faith. It shows all the battles, trials and tribulations that mankind experiences throughout the ages and it doesn't pull any punches. It shows all the attributes and flaws in the character of man, unlike so many ancient writings where famous Kings for example, have wanted to leave their own interpretation of their legacy on history, even though it was less than the truth. The Bible, on the other hand presents the hard facts about people who struggle with life, with themselves, and with a loving God who constantly calls them to live under the wing of His protection but in accordance with His laws. Through it all we see mankind wanting to live as he pleases, in his foolishness, pride and arrogance despite God's laws being for the good of all. It is the one place where we can find out who we are, why we came to be born, what our purpose is here on earth and about the incredible future that awaits all those who accept the law of God made flesh in Jesus for everyone to see. In the book of John Chapter 16, verse 33: Jesus tells us that we will all have troubles in this world because that is what life is about, but he also told us that he has overcome the world and so can we, if we have asked him to live in us by his spirit. The Bible shows us clearly that evil exists and that no matter how much people may wish to ridicule this reality as a fairy tale, there is a spiritual opposition that we must come to terms with. This opposition is an enemy called the devil or Satan whose aim is to keep us involved with sin. We must decide whether we believe what the Bible tells us in this regard or not. If we refuse God's offer of salvation and freedom from sin, then we should not be surprised with our continual involvement with sin. But the Bible tells us that once we have received the spirit of Christ Jesus into our lives, we are born again and the Holy Spirit of God will heighten our conscience, providing all that we need to prevent ourselves from falling into sin.

"Whosoever is born of God doth not commit sin; for his seed remaineth in him: and he cannot sin, because he is born of God." (1John 3:9)

Once Christians are born again, we have moved from the kingdom of darkness to the kingdom of light; but if we purpose to live the holy life God desires and witness for Him, we will enter into a war against Satan and that which causes us to sin – Iniquity. We begin to understand that there is a constant war going on in the heavenly realms that affects everyone here on the earth.

'For we wrestle not against flesh and blood, but against principalities, against powers, against the rulers of the darkness of this world, against spiritual wickedness in high places.' (Ephesians 6:12)

Satan's aim, above all things, is to prevent us from coming to know the truth about Jesus, and furthermore, when we do, to ensure that we remain as ineffective as possible in our part to play bringing God's Kingdom to fruition. The Bible explains that from the moment of birth, we are born into the midst of a great spiritual battle and we come into the world without the spirit of God indwelling us. It explains that this means we are born into *iniquity: i.e.* we are born naturally into a state of selfishness and rebellion against God. Anyone who doubts this needs only to watch babies. The reality is, that as they grow up, babies need to be trained to do what is right because they don't have a problem doing the exact opposite quite naturally. Therefore, we come into the world separated from God and unless we come into relationship with the one who made us and who wants a relationship with us, we will continue with this inbuilt desire to live for ourselves throughout our existence.

Perhaps one of the most amazing facts the Bible teaches is that due the spread of sin throughout the earth, Satan, who is described as a mighty fallen angel, with enormous power, is now in control of the world. WHAT, I hear you say? How could this possibly be true? Because the Bible confirms it. It is a mystery but also part of God's great redemptive plan for mankind.

'We know that we are children of God, and that the whole world is under the control of the evil one.' (1John 5:19)

When sin entered the world through man's conscious rebellion against God's laws, the world was set on a pathway for future mankind to sin. As sin increases, so the whole world comes under the power of sin. God has clearly told us, that in this world there will always be the temptation *(comes from Satan)* to live for ourselves, and this will entail sins that emanate from the iniquity or disease that we are born with. The fact is, that there is a

191

spiritual being called Satan, and he is an enemy of God. The Bible tells us that he is an angelic being of great power who wants to be worshipped as God. Furthermore, that he will achieve this for a period of time, before Jesus returns. He is real and his job is to destroy faith in God. He will do it in every conceivable way. Jesus called him a liar and the great deceiver. He will speak into our minds and lie, deceive, play on our pride and our arrogance. He knows how to provoke the very worst in humanity, anger, jealousy and hate and even murder. He is an expert, and he will do everything he can to bring doubt to a believer in God and to prevent people from coming into God's Kingdom. The most common doubt will always be, *"Did God really say?"* It is amazing how easily this seems to work! All sins are nothing more than the working out of our own desires and lusts caused by the iniquity within and aided by this spiritual being who wills us to do so.

But we must understand something really important. Satan is NOT omnipresent like God, so he can't be everywhere at the same time, as can God. But he has an army that affects us from the moment we wake up each day. Whether we want to believe it or not, the Bible tells us that Satan is in command of millions and millions of demons who do his bidding. But neither Satan nor his demons can read our thoughts as can God. He can only play on our weaknesses and he is an expert at doing just that. So, he constantly whispers to us all sorts of lies about any number of situations. The Bible tells us that he is the great tempter and he will lie about God and about who we are. In the natural, we see this worked out in the people we relate to, either at home or at work or in church. We will experience confusion due to false truths being expounded in day to day situations. What we experience in the natural is the outworking of what happening in the spiritual realms. (*Anyone who wants to know more about how Satan and his demons operate should read the book by C.S Lewis, called 'The Screwtape Letters'*).

As a result, humans also lie, steal and murder and are capable of committing the worst atrocities imaginable. Despite this, humans still struggle to believe in evil and cannot comprehend where it comes from. However, I haven't found one single person who can give me a better, more grounded and sensible reason for the presence of evil other than that offered in the Bible.

Standing Firm

But, thank God, we are given all the armaments required to stand against the temptation to sin:

"Finally, my brethren, be strong in the Lord, and in the power of his might. Put on the whole armour of God, that ye may be able to stand against the wiles of the devil. For we wrestle not against flesh and blood, but against principalities, against powers, against the rulers of the darkness of this world, against spiritual wickedness in high places. Wherefore take unto you the whole armour of God, that ye may be able to withstand in the evil day, and having done all, to stand. Stand therefore, having your loins girt about with truth, and having on the breastplate

of righteousness; And your feet shod with the preparation of the gospel of peace; Above all, taking the shield of faith, wherewith ye shall be able to quench all the fiery darts of the wicked. And take the helmet of salvation, and the sword of the Spirit, which is the word of God: Praying always with all prayer and supplication in the Spirit, and watching thereunto with all perseverance and supplication for all saints". (Ephesians 6:10-18)

The scripture above needs to be considered in much detail but regrettably is often glossed over. Each of these items of armour is imperative if we are to survive and flourish in this fallen world and become effective for God. However, there are times when we do fail and Christians can fall into sin. But the Bible tells us that if we do fall into sin, we have one to whom we can approach to seek forgiveness each and every moment of the day. God then sets us on a new path.

If we confess our sins, he is faithful and just and will forgive us our sins and purify us from all unrighteousness. (1John 1:9)

But, we are not supposed to somehow just accept sin in our lives; we are to be in a constant state of awareness about our propensity to sin. If we do continue to sin, the Bible says that only Holy Spirit can convict us and bring us to repentance. But if we resist this calling, the Bible teaches that there is a price to pay:

Converging Signs and Rejection of Truth

'For if we sin wilfully after that we have received the knowledge of the truth there remains no more sacrifice for sins. '(Hebrews 10:26)

So, I have to ask, are you born again of God? Have you actually asked God for forgiveness for your own resistance to Him and asked Jesus Christ to indwell you by His spirit? What happens if we are not? Maybe we would prefer not to face such questions. Maybe we might simply believe that we will somehow be OK. If that rings true, then I suggest you may have lost sight of the true gospel that Jesus died for and the importance of what it means to prepare ourselves for Jesus' Second Coming. It may, in fact, be a prompt by the Holy Spirit to re-think our priorities in life! Whether we like it or not, the consequences for sin are serious. By accepting Jesus as our Lord and Saviour, we are given the gift of life through new birth and the power to sin no more.

'There was a man of the Pharisees, named Nicodemus, a ruler of the Jews: The same came to Jesus by night, and said unto him, Rabbi, we know that thou art a teacher come from God: for no man can do these miracles that thou doest, except God be with him. Jesus answered and said unto him, Verily, verily, I say unto thee, Except a man be born again, he cannot see the kingdom of God. Nicodemus saith unto him, How can a man be born when he is old? can he enter the second time into his mother's womb, and be born? Jesus answered, Verily, verily, I say unto thee, Except a man be born of water and of the Spirit, he cannot enter into the kingdom of God. That which is born of the flesh is flesh; and that which is born

195

of the Spirit is spirit. Marvel not that I said unto thee, Ye must be born again. The wind bloweth where it listeth, and thou hearest the sound thereof, but canst not tell whence it cometh, and whither it goeth: so is every one that is born of the Spirit. (John 3:1-8

Jesus offers an amazing gift of life to all those who accept him as their Lord and Saviour. We will still live in this world and be subject to all the trials and tribulations one can imagine and this includes a constant battle with iniquity. We are in a world where sin can govern everything that happens each and every day. We are faced with a world of people whose natural inclination is to disobey God and His laws. The consequences should be obvious! But God gives us the power to resist all sin as we seek to be obedient to his Word.

Being an 'Overcomer'

Those of us who do find truth in Jesus will soon begin to understand the nature of spiritual war, but others who choose to deny this reality will remain unaware because they are no threat to Satan's kingdom on the earth. This may all sound very much like fairy-tale land, but for anyone who really wants to find out whether this battle is real or not, they need only seek out Christians who can testify to this amazing 'new birth' experience that totally changed their lives. The sheer number and similarity in stories is very convincing. The Bible tells us clearly what evil is. However, God's promise remains firm. In John 3: 12 -20 Jesus says:

"If I have told you earthly things, and ye believe not, how shall ye believe, if I tell you of heavenly things? And no man hath ascended up to heaven, but he that came down from heaven, even the Son of man which is in heaven. And as Moses lifted up the serpent in the wilderness, even so must the Son of man be lifted up: That whosoever believeth in him should not perish, but have eternal life. For God so loved the world, that he gave his only begotten Son, that whosoever believeth in him should not perish, but have everlasting life. For God sent not his Son into the world to condemn the world; but that the world through him might be saved. He that believeth on him is not condemned: but he that believeth not is condemned already, because he hath not believed in the name of the only begotten Son of God. And this is the condemnation, that light is come into the world, and men loved darkness rather than light, because their deeds were evil. For every one that doeth evil hateth the light, neither cometh to the light, lest his deeds should be reproved."

Jesus tells us that by believing in God and receiving his spirit we would have all that we need to overcome this spiritual battle. From that moment, Satan would have no power over us unless we choose to give it to him. God would give us the strength through Christ, to carry on whatever the circumstances. We overcome because he has already overcome through the cross:

"These things I have spoken unto you, that in me ye might have peace. In the world ye shall have tribulation: but be of good cheer; I have overcome the world." (John 16:33)

Converging Signs and Rejection of Truth

Knowing who you are as Darkness Falls

Today, we are entering the last of the last days spoken about in the Bible, which will engulf Christians in the most intense spiritual battle ever known. We will need to know who we are in Christ. Amongst all the signs that are manifesting themselves, we will witness people feeling less and less able to even speak publicly without fear of reprisal by heavy-handed governments who will continue introducing laws that will become more and more draconian. Whatever we might think, political correctness has become a serious problem, with hate laws being introduced that can stop nearly everyone from even expressing a view about anything or anyone. But Jesus said that 'anyone' who chooses to be his disciple *will* suffer persecution.

As I have already mentioned, the Canadian Clinical Psychologist Professor Jordan Peterson is a new voice to millions of people but he is currently experiencing such persecution. He has been given the gift to be able to articulate clearly what so many people feel today about the 'spirit of the age' and the dangers of political correctness and signs of extreme authoritarianism sweeping across the Western nations. In his widely attended lectures, he speaks regularly about the need to understand that there is such a thing as absolute truth but he also knows that it is under serious threat in our postmodernistic, politically driven society. He appears to understans only too well that there has, over the last 20 years or so, been a complete breakdown in trust amongst most people groups, whose moral compass, once based on the origin of ancient laws instigated by God, has now been severely compromised. Like journalist Melanie Phillips he believes that we, in the Western world, have primarily become a Godless society. What does this mean? Quite simply that we have chosen to deny the truth. It is actually a wilful denial of truth that places us once again, in Satan's territory whether we choose to believe he is real or not. We should therefore expect all that will inevitably follow. We can read what God says about this in the book of Romans:

"Wherefore God also gave them up to uncleanness through the lusts of their own hearts, to dishonour their own bodies between themselves: Who changed the truth of God into a lie, and worshipped and served the creature more than the Creator, who is blessed for ever. Amen".
(Romans 1:24-25)

A Powerful Delusion is Coming

The Bible teaches that a time is coming when God will send a powerful delusion over the earth that will prevent people from coming to know him.

"And for this cause God shall send them strong delusion, that they should believe a lie:

This may seem very extreme and hardly what we might expect from a loving God but there is a reason. In the book of 2 Thessalonians Chapter 2:11 we read:

'That they all might be damned who believed not the truth, but had pleasure in unrighteousness.'

Paul explains in these verses that it is because people have decided in their hearts that they simply do not want to know the truth. It is a 'heart' matter. This is a terrible situation in which to find oneself, just at the same time that the man of sin, the Anti-Christ is rising to fool all people groups into believing that he is the return of the Messiah - The Christ! Those who refuse this gift of salvation in Christ are in serious spiritual danger.

Chapter 11: What Type of Church for the Days that Lie Ahead?

In the light of the accuracy of Bible prophecy to date, it is important to pose the question; why are so few Christians not bringing a wider sense of awareness about prophecies that are being fulfilled in our time to those who lack any sense of hope for the future? I am forced to conclude that this is because so few seem to have any understanding themselves, having had little, if any teaching from their local church leaders for probably over 50 years. I know of many Christians who have said that they cannot recall ever having received any teaching from the prophetic books of the Bible and particularly the book of Revelation in their local churches. This is all the more disturbing in the light of the fact that Jesus specifically told us that we would be blessed by hearing his last words from this book. This sad omission is confirmed by most older, more mature Christians, who agree that during the past 50 years or so, the church in the Western world has received little teaching about the end times, eschatology (*Eschatos*) meaning the 'last' and (*logy*) meaning 'the study of'. End times theology is concerned with the final events of history, or the ultimate destiny of humankind. For centuries, eschatological doctrine was always a part of the teaching the whole of scripture. So, what has happened over the past 50 years or so years to have caused church leaders to have seemingly rejected such teaching? The answer is that something spiritual in nature has captured our attention. This is very noticeable when dialoguing with Christians who have not received any eschatological teaching. It all too often, seems to cause many to assume that we are somehow speaking about fairy tales, or conspiracy theories, or something that is in the very distant future, about which we need not concern ourselves. It is clear that there are spiritual reasons for this omission in teaching. This is none other than Satan deceiving the world and the church as we draw closer to Jesus Second Coming in these last days. In the period leading up to this event, Jesus main warning focussed directly on the increase in deception. He specifically said that there would be a great falling away (Apostasy) from the Christian faith caused by the rise of an anti-Christ spirit and this would increase as we drew closer to the end.

Now, more than ever, is the time when church leaders everywhere need to consider what is happening in the world and be teaching from the prophetic scriptures in order to bring a sense of real hope to a dying world. I have always been convinced that the church is the answer to the world, but, at the same time, I have struggled with the reality that 'church' has so often been such a stumbling block. It is only through the church that God can speak to lost people who are in desperate need of truth during these times. But to do this, the church must be prepared and there is a desperate need for local church leaders to bring effective teaching. In this chapter, I want to outline what I believe will identify what the true church of Christ is and what it will need to be in the days that lie ahead.

Before doing so, I would like to clarify the meaning of the word 'church', although I believe Jesus was absolutely clear about his intentions for his church. The term 'church', comes from the Greek word, 'Ecclesia' meaning *called out ones*. The true 'church' will be made up from those who have recognised the sacrificial love of Jesus Christ through his death on the cross to pay the price for sin, his resurrection to physical life and the impartation of the Holy Spirit to his followers to empower them to live the Christian life. The moment the Holy Spirit convicts us about the sin our own lives and we recognise what Jesus did for us, we can receive forgiveness. It is then, that we are, as Jesus says, born again of the spirit of God. We are re-connected with God once again and have the privilege of having a daily relationship with Jesus. Only these 'called out ones' will be able to see clearly the difference between truth and lies. Everyone else who holds on to 'religion' or 'tradition' will be deceived just as Jesus told us they would. I believe that as we move through these last days, only the true church of Christ will be able to take a stand against the forces of evil that are coming upon us. I am therefore forced to conclude that this 'true church' may look quite different from that which most of us might have in our minds. It will be determined by the quality of relationships where people meet 'spirit to spirit' in truth and vulnerability, where people really care for one another, practically and above all spiritually. It will be what marks out those who will give one another up from those who will stand together to the end, even unto death

It is clear that church, as most Christians understand it, generally comprises of weekly Sunday meetings to meet together to worship God and receive His word (The Bible) into our lives as well as meeting occasionally in small groups. However, the issue is, what is the spiritual connection between believers in the quality of their relationships and what is being taught?

For example, when I was investigating joining the Anglican ministry, after I became a Christian, I was told that people don't have the ability to concentrate for more than 18 minutes at a time. Sermons, as they were called, were therefore restricted to this timeframe. In other church mainstreams, the times may differ, but generally speaking this is the amount of time given to people hearing the word of God in the Anglican church, if indeed the word of God is preached at all. All too often, one may end up listening to the thoughts of a church minister about his specific understanding of life and society, with only the minimum of attention paid to the word of God. There is no response from the congregation.

In other streams, for example the Pentecostal churches, one might very well find the sermon or 'talk' lasting for at least an hour, during which time it is always possible to tell whether people are engaged with what is being said and agreeing to it, if members of the congregation shout out 'Hallelujah' or 'Amen'. Both my wife and I have most certainly received much inspiring preaching and teaching over the years that I am sure has spurred us on in our Christian service, but I have to say that most of it has come from attendance at specific churches occasionally visited, Christian Conferences, and on the Internet where it is possible to hear strong, Biblically sound teachers. I think it is clear that unless the word of God dwells richly within, Christians will not have the inner drive to become fully devoted members of Christ's body. Moreover, they are unlikely to be prepared for the Second Coming of Jesus. In this chapter, I wanted to challenge Christians, church leaders and their congregations to consider what kind of church Jesus is expecting to find when he comes again.

What are marks of a True Church of Jesus Christ

What are the marks of a church that must demonstrate its faithfulness to Christ in making disciples who go into all the world as he commanded? What will make such disciples distinctive during times of persecution in the days that lie ahead? Before we try to answer these questions, we need to face the fact that Jesus did prophesy that as we enter into the times of tribulation, there would be a great falling away from the Christian faith into a state of apostasy? He even asked the question that when he returns, would even find faith on the earth!

"Nevertheless, when the Son of man cometh, shall he find faith on the earth?" (Luke 18:8)

I believe that in the days to come, only those churches who recognise the signs of the times and the rise of evil that will propel the anti-Christ into power will be able to fulfil the requirements of Jesus in preparing the body of Christ for his Second Coming.

I am going to list 13 marks that I believe will distinguish the true church from the false apostate church:

Church that understands the times - no compromise with evil
Have Western Christian Nations been lulled into a false sense of security? This is exactly what happened leading up to the Second World War, when the German people knew Hitler was on the rise. Germany was a nation where Christianity had been thoroughly integrated into the whole population over a period of four hundred years or so. It was a country of 'Lutherans with a strong Roman Catholic population, seemingly very disciplined in their Christian faith. Surely, of all nations, this was a nation of people who could have recognised sheer evil when it saw it?

Dietrich Bonhoeffer, the famous young pastor and theologian, was said to have commented that if more

German people had simply read Adolf Hitler's book *Mein Kampf*, written in 1925, many years before he actually came to power, they would have seen only too clearly what he believed and stood for and would never have allowed him to become Chancellor. Bonhoeffer was one of a very few Christian leaders who did everything he could to warn the church about the evil that was coming over the land. In the book *Pastor, Martyr, Prophet, Spy*, it was Bonhoeffer who said that you could not compromise with sheer evil and he was right.

We can read about his desperate plight to get the German people and the UK Government, as well as the Church in England, to see what was manifesting in their very midst. But throughout it all, the church leaders of the day wanted to believe that God, through his love and grace, would surely answer their prayers and bring the light of truth to Adolf Hitler. Bonhoeffer was imprisoned for some time just before he was to be married and finally murdered by the Nazis at age 33. How ironic and sad that someone so on fire with the truth of the scriptures, working so hard to warn the people, should have been murdered by the Nazis just a matter of months before Hitler committed suicide and the Second World War was over.

In the United Kingdom it seemed that few people had the authority, courage, tenacity and influence to bring a warning to a gullible United Kingdom Parliament about the coming rise of sheer evil. But Winston Churchill saw the seriousness of the situation, recognising it for what it was. He stood firm in what had to be done. Amazingly, we are reminded about this momentous time in history in the film called *'The Darkest Hour'*. God, in His mercy, used Winston Churchill at the most important time in history. During the film, when others were trying to persuade Churchill to compromise with the evil, he bellowed, *"You don't compromise with a tiger when it has your head in its mouth."*

The question is, will church leaders and their congregations in the Western church realise before it is too late that they cannot afford to compromise any more with Satan who has its head in his mouth?

Church with Sound Doctrine and 'Grace Filled'

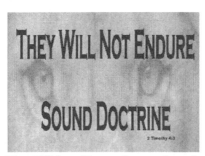

The doctrines of the Bible are simply the teachings of God's word, which is a book of doctrine. Take doctrine out of God's word and you have nothing left! The Bible tells us that a time is coming when people will not put up with sound doctrine. In the Bible we read:

"For the time will come when people will not put up with sound doctrine. Instead, to suit their own desires, they

will gather around them a great number of teachers to say what their itching ears want to hear" (2Timothy 4:3)

This means that people will not want to hear truth. They will want to hear things that will soothe their stresses in life. We are told the same in Isaiah 30:10, where we see the people wanting to hear 'smooth' or 'pleasant' things :

"See no more visions!" and to the prophets, *"Give us no more visions of what is right! Tell us pleasant things, prophesy illusions or deceits."*

Amazing isn't it? That people would actually say that they did not want to hear truth, because they prefer to live lives of illusion! But this is happening now and it is leading to many rejecting the Christian gospel and it will lead to a time of 'tribulation' like no other.

For this reason, therefore, the church for the days that lie ahead will be one that places a heavy emphasis of the teaching of sound doctrine, declared in the love and grace of Christ. Today, in so many churches there is little emphasis on delivering sound doctrine at all. In fact, some church members ask, 'What is doctrine?' The answer is purely teaching honestly and accurately what is written in the Bible as opposed to teaching what someone may think it says. It is the difference between what is called *exegesis:* that which extracts from the scriptures what they actually say and *eisegesis:* that which is emphasises your own point of view, using scripture to do so. It is also ensuring that teaching is in accordance with the signs of the times because people need to know how to apply doctrine in the midst of their daily lives. Without sound Biblical doctrine, the body of Christ will be unable to stand in the face of the coming persecution that so many other Christians suffer across the world. At present, so many Christians reach a state of pseudo spirituality, but it has no real power to live the Christian life.

Church of New Birth in Christ

In John Chapter 3, verse 3, Jesus told the Pharisee Nicodemus that he needed to be born again to be able to see the Kingdom of God,

"Verily, verily, I say unto thee, except a man be born again, he cannot see the kingdom of God"

This means that only those who experience this new birth in Christ can demonstrate that inner drive that comes from the indwelling of the Holy Spirit that enables them to swim in the right direction. This inner experience is the confirmation that a new creation has been formed by God through Jesus Christ. It is only through this new birth experience that we can rely on the fact that they will be led by the Holy Spirit. What are we to make of those who purport to be Christians who show no such drive or desire. Those who have little interest in even reading the Bible, let alone doing what it says? As it says in the book of James 1:22

"But be ye doers of the word, and not hearers only, deceiving your own selves"

Should such Christians without this inner drive feel personally guilty? Stan Firth, a retired Christian pastor, in his book *'Custom and Command'* believes that many so-called new births are not real and that these people have become victims of certain styles of evangelism or leadership that has made participation in church activities

the thermometer for commitment to Christ. I suppose that I have always felt this to be true because I believe that only a spirit led birth can generally create an inner thirst and desire to know absolute truth which then drives them as a New Creature in Christ into the Scriptures and the desire to meet together constantly so that they may grow as Christians into the likeness of Christ.

"Therefore, if anyone is in Christ, the new creation has come. The old has gone, the new is here!" (2 Corinthians 5:17) *"Instead, speaking the truth in love, we will grow to become in every respect the mature body of him who is the head, that is, Christ"* (Ephesians 4:15).

In the book of Acts chapter 2, verses 40-47 we read that the new believers accepted the message of salvation and repentance and this resulted in an amazing change as they suddenly felt a sense of fear (awesome sense of the magnificence and power of God) of the Lord that totally changed their lives:

"And with many other words did he testify and exhort, saying, Save yourselves from this untoward generation. Then they that gladly received his word were baptized: and the same day there were added unto them about three thousand souls. And they continued steadfastly in the apostles' doctrine and fellowship, and in breaking of bread, and in prayers. And fear came upon every soul: and many wonders and signs were done by the apostles. And all that believed were together and had all things common; And sold their possessions and goods, and parted them to all men, as every man had need. And they, continuing daily with one accord in the temple, and breaking bread from house to house, did eat their meat with gladness and singleness of heart, Praising God, and having favour with all the people. And the Lord added to the church daily such as should be saved."

The emphasis in this scripture is: continuing steadfast in doctrine and fellowship, breaking of bread and prayer. I believe that we are going to experience this type of Christian new birth much more in the days that lie ahead but it will probably come out of persecution. However, my concerns are that structured church will not always meet their needs, because you cannot mix Christians and non-Christians together for worship or spiritual fellowship.

"Be ye not unequally yoked together with unbelievers: for what fellowship hath righteousness with unrighteousness?

And what communion hath light with darkness? (2 Corinthians 6:14)

This is not to say that Christians should not mix with non-Christians; of course they should, but that they cannot expect to share the same spirit, especially in such troubled times.

"I wrote to you in my letter not to associate with sexually immoral people —not at all meaning the people of this world who are immoral, or the greedy and swindlers, or idolaters. In that case you would have to leave this world." (1 Corinthians 5: 9-10)

"Be wise in the way you act toward outsiders; make the most of every opportunity. Let your conversation be always full of grace, seasoned with salt, so that you may know how to answer everyone." (Colossians 4:5-6)

Church that is Spirit-Filled and Mission Orientated

The church able to stand in the days that lie ahead will comprise of those filled with the Spirit of God, who love each other and who love God. It will be one that God adds to their number those who are being saved. They will be a community of believers who come together to pray for the purposes of God to be fulfilled in these days. It will be one with strong prayerful Christians who can discern what is going on in the heavenly realms and who can see with God's wisdom what is taking place in the spiritual battle we are in the midst of. It will comprise of Christians who come together to worship God and who utilise the gifts of the Spirit in encouraging one another as they serve the purposes of God, especially in reaching out with the message of the Gospel to the community.

It is interesting to note that so many people use the scripture in Hebrews 10:25, out of context in trying to encourage Christians to continue to worship together in Sunday church services.

'And let us consider one another to provoke unto love and to good works: Not forsaking the assembling of ourselves together, as the manner of some is; but exhorting one another: and so much the more, as ye see the day approaching.'

Again, Stan Firth points out in his book that Sundays have become a custom and they are certainly not commanded in the Scriptures; hence the title of the book *'Custom and Command'*. He believes worship times in church services in many evangelical churches have invariably become the construction or creation of ourselves that so often seem to lack any genuine connection with the living God.

Over the past twenty years or so, it seems that services in so many Charismatic churches have been constructed to flow as if we have been seeking ways to persuade God to manifest His presence amongst us with 'signs and wonders' in the hope that this will encourage us to carry on living out Christian lives more dynamically. Whilst not wanting to belittle this desire, I believe that true worship is actually a spontaneous response of the appreciation and love for God and His love for us. It is a lifestyle and an understanding that God is in everything we do and that if we have eyes to see, we are able to identify precious moments which enable us to appreciate him, that bring us into a sense of worship. So, the question remains, is attending a regular organised 'worship service' each week worshipping God? Many people will say yes, but others say that the scriptures tell us that where two or three are gathered together in genuine open fellowship, Jesus is in our midst and that this is church.

Reading the New Testament certainly challenges our understanding about how we currently 'do' church but we need to differentiate between our church traditions and functions and to try to determine what it is really like to 'be' church to each other. How should we consider various areas of 'church life' that would include baptism, church discipline and accountability and, of course, the ministries that are there to build up the body of Christ as described in Ephesians chapter 4: verse 11 onwards. These are issues that many Christians have struggled with for years. The question is, can they all not also be achieved within an unstructured church environment and lifestyle? I believe they can, and more can be learned from a variety of Christian leaders, writers and authors who have ventured down this path, some successfully and others not. The problem is that we have been dealing with our structured interpretation of church for centuries and to consider anything out of the ordinary is always difficult.

Converging Signs and Rejection of Truth

One thing is for sure, I do believe that the 'faithful church' for the days that lie ahead will be able to stand against persecution and remain firm in an age when the anti-Christ Spirit increases in power. This will be because it will have been grounded in the Word of God and is moving in the full power of the Holy Spirit, experiencing real spiritual relationships that will be closer and more intimate than those we see today in the majority of churches. Christians will really trust one another not to give one another up when persecution comes (Matthew 24:10), even to the point of death. This may sound very melodramatic in our very warm and cosy Western style of Christianity that has remained as yet unchallenged by any form of major persecution or government decree until now. It is clear, however, that we have entered times where it is difficult to maintain the concept of free speech with laws being introduced that may actually prevent us from even being able to think out loud, let alone speak. The idea that making a statement that can be construed as affecting people's feelings and therefore warranting legal proceedings against another person, is not something that we should accept. And yet, this is the pathway that the laws of this land have created. We need the return of Acts 2 Church.

Church Led by the Prophetic

As 'The World' faces up to the enormous challenges outlined in earlier chapters, I only wish I could say the same about the church. Unfortunately, so many churches and their leaders are much like the world and moving in the same direction. Instead of church leaders recognising the seriousness and the significance of prophetic events, it all too often seems that they choose to believe in unity of all things. The Bible does tell us that one day this will be so, but not yet; instead, the book of Revelation teaches that this earth will be destroyed by fire and God will then recreate a new heaven and a new earth and only then will there be perfect harmony.

"And I saw a new heaven and a new earth: for the first heaven and the first earth were passed away; and there was no more sea. And I John saw the holy city, new Jerusalem, coming down from God out of heaven, prepared as a bride adorned for her husband. And I heard a great voice out of heaven saying, Behold, the tabernacle of God is with men, and he will dwell with them, and they shall be his people, and God himself shall be with them, and be their God. And God shall wipe away all tears from their eyes; and there shall be no more death, neither sorrow, nor crying, neither shall there be any more pain: for the former things are passed away.

And he that sat upon the throne said, Behold, I make all things new. And he said unto me, Write: for these words are true and faithful. And he said unto me, It is done. I am Alpha and Omega, the beginning and the end. I will give unto him that is athirst of the fountain of the water of life freely.

⁷ He that overcometh shall inherit all things; and I will be his God, and he shall be my son." Revelation 21:1-7

What an amazing prospect for all those 'overcomers' in Christ who have lived lives honouring to God and who have come through the times of tribulation that may have even involved death. Surely this will be the most joyful time and one that every person on the earth would like to be a part of? But at present, despite the urgency of the times, there appears to be little understanding about the need to prepare God's people in the light of what is happening all around us.

In many ways, it is somewhat ironic that as governments and economists failed to bring any warnings before the 2008 world financial crisis, most church leaders are today failing to recognise the signs pointing to the return of Christ and the need to prepare. So, the question is – is there a source that can be trusted to provide an understanding of what the world and the church faces in the days to come? The answer is emphatically yes – it's the Bible.

The Bible is full of prophecy. In the book *'Countdown to Calamity or Hope for the Future'* written by Tony Pearce, he, like and many others who study prophecy, states that over a quarter of the verses in the Bible contain prophecy. That of the 31,124 verses in the Bible 1,219 in the Old Testament contain predictions and of the 7,914 verses in the New Testament, 1,711 are predictions. He estimates that 27% of the entire Bible is prophecy. The Bible also shows the prophecies that have already been fulfilled, those in the process of happening now and some yet to be fulfilled. If we simply look at the prophecies that have been fulfilled we will find that they have been 100%

accurate, so why should we not have confidence that those which have not yet happened will be in the future?

The Bible, after all, has been proven to be more reliable than any other ancient text. There is an enormous amount of manuscript evidence for the New Testament as we know it today, way beyond any other ancient document. We have over 24,000 manuscript copies of portions of the New Testament in existence today. No other document of antiquity even begins to approach such numbers and attestation. In fact, quotations from the New Testament in early Christian writings are so extensive that it could virtually be reconstructed from these writings without the use of the New Testament manuscripts. There are no less than 39,000 quotations from the New Testament in the works of early Christian writers. These include Irenaeus, Clement of Alexandra, Tertullian, Hippolytus and Eusebius. (Information from 'Evidence that demands a verdict' by Josh McDowell.

In the New Testament Peter wrote:

*'Moreover, we possess the prophetic word as an altogether reliable thing. You do well if you pay attention to this as you would to a light shining in a murky place, until the day dawns and the morning star rises in your hearts. Above all, you do well if you recognize this: No prophecy of scripture ever comes about by the prophet's own imagination, for no prophecy was ever borne of human impulse; rather, men carried along by the Holy Spirit spoke from God.' (*2Peter 1:19-21)

Tony Pearce also has an excellent web site called *'Light for the Last Days'* that is well worth visiting. You will find it is packed with very detailed teaching. There are also many other sources that do the same, like Jacob Prasch for example, who, being a converted Jew, has studied what the prophecies mean from a Jewish perspective. In his books 'Harpazo', 'Shadows of the Beast' and 'The Dilemma of Laodicea', he teaches very clearly about prophecy and end time events. I am not, therefore, going to try and duplicate what so many eminent scholars have already written.

One thing is sure, throughout the Old Testament, whenever God's people wanted to go their own way, calling for smooth or pleasant prophecies to suit their 'itching ears', God would always raise His prophets to call them back to the right pathway. The question is, will the church in the West hear the voices that God has raised up to speak about the need to prepare in the days in which we are currently living? Will you, the reader, hear and act?

In reality, we have been witnessing this 'spirit of the age' rapidly drawing us towards Biblical destiny for many years. During this time, its influence has turned people away from God and towards their own lustful desires with some very clever but deceptive ideas and beliefs. After a move of God during the late 1960s and 1970s, when the Charismatic renewal was born, thousands of people became Christians, many in stadiums where the late Billy

Graham preached. Since then, we have seen the satanic spirit gradually bring a strong influence that persuades millions towards 'another gospel' and away from the true and living God, although most do not see it because it appears to be so lifelike. This has seriously reduced the effectiveness of the church in these days.

Many previously faithful churches and their leaders have been beguiled into believing that although we are going through worldly difficulties, we are still on the right track towards building the church that Jesus came to die for. Nothing seems to have changed in their eyes. Yes, most realise that the world faces some serious problems, but they have been trained, in the main, to believe in a post millennial view of the future, without even realising it. For many leaders who have bought into this relativistic world, this primarily means there is no such thing as absolute truth. Many do not, in fact, really adhere to a literal understanding of the millennial reign of Christ in any case. Instead, they believe that through faith in the signs and wonders ministry, the world can be brought to the knowledge of Christ ready for his eventual return. This often referred to as 'Dominionism', a view held by many leaders who now subscribe to the 'Emergent Church' that is also redefining the meaning of the basic doctrines of the Bible. This new breed of leaders and some from evangelical backgrounds that held to basic doctrine, believe that by taking hold of the signs and wonders ministry, the church can take hold of the world ruled by Satan and win it for Christ before he comes again. As a result, they effectively nullify the prophetic scriptures. They seem to think they know where they are going, even if many admit that they don't really concern themselves with Biblical prophecy anymore.

Very few pastors and teachers appear to regard Biblical prophecy as important and some even believe that their congregations should avoid it, and focus instead, on evangelism and helping a world in distress. Unfortunately, so many leaders have therefore failed to preach from the prophetic scriptures in any meaningful way about the 'signs of the times'. The fact that the book of Revelation consists of the last words of Jesus to His church doesn't seem important! People are often told that this book is simply too difficult to understand or that it needs to be interpreted figuratively or mystically despite the fact that it is the only book where Jesus tells us that we will be blessed as we hear his words. The fact that the whole theme of prophecy throughout the Bible is leading us towards the end times doesn't seem to be preached anymore.

Church that values Expository Preaching

The church in the West today experiences much less expository preaching than was once the case. Nowadays, preaching comprises much motivational speaking that inspires people for a moment but has no lasting impact. The Bible says that it is the power of the gospel that brings people to the knowledge of God and true salvation. The order of the day now seems to consist of presenting an inspiring talk that is often devoid of doctrine which can actually change lives. Such talks may be peppered with a number of scriptures, but these are so often taken completely out of context and only introduced to further a point that the speaker wishes to make rather than to exegete what the scripture actually teaches. Strong Biblical doctrine or prophecy is often completely overlooked and the power of the scripture is lost and devoid of any possibility of the Holy Spirit being able to minister to our inner souls. Today, preaching that changes people's lives is getting harder to find in local churches.

The death of the world's most famous evangelist, Billy Graham at age 99 was announced this year. In the various media reports about his life and ministry, it was interesting to note the comments in a number of Christian news articles that his preaching in later life lacked the same degree of fervour about the consequences of sin that he preached in his early years. It is perhaps even more interesting to learn that some mainstream news writers indicated that as he began to mix with politicians and world leaders, there was a need to tone down what was considered to be 'the extreme nature' of the Christian Gospel.

This is not intended to be a criticism in any way because who knows what any of us might be held accountable for when we meet the Lord after our death? I just believe that everyone should watch Billy Graham preaching to the thousands at Wembley in 1957 to be reminded of the power of the gospel. What a great 'preach' this was. You will find it on You Tube. I recently played this video to a Christian leader who commented afterwards that he wondered if Billy Graham could have got away with such a preach in today's society? I wonder indeed!

Church that Preaches the whole of Scripture

I believe that sooner rather than later, a decision is going to have to be made by all church leaders to consider the strength and impact of the gospel preached in their own churches. They will need to decide whether they are inadvertently, bringing 'another gospel' that might simply incorporate weekly motivational talks that are insufficient to save or to change lives. To consider whether the gospel will save will not only include the message of God's love, forgiveness and compassion, but also be one that speaks about the iniquity man is born with that causes sin that leads to physical and spiritual death.

Such churches must review whether they are preaching the gospel that speaks of repentance; one that leads to life as we are born again from above. A gospel that confirms there are real places called heaven and hell and teaches of our need to eagerly await the Second coming of Christ, after which it will be too late for decision. A gospel that confirms when Christ returns just as he promised, he will remove the faithful, true church in what is called the rapture (*harpazo*) leaving all those who refused the truth to face the Wrath of God. A gospel that confirms Jesus will reign as King of Kings on the earth for a thousand years together with all Christians who return to reign with him during this Millennial reign. A gospel that speaks of the culmination of history, where every person who has ever lived will come before the judgement seat of God in what is called the great last day White Throne final judgement. A gospel that confirms the re-making of a new heaven and a new earth, where those who are in Christ will live with our father God for eternity. This is the decision church leaders will need to make if we are to see those that God is drawing to himself saved in these last days. Everything else will be insufficient to enable Christians to stand.

Church Ready for Persecution

 A church ready for persecution, will be one that has been tested and understands that persecution has been the historic basis for church growth. Persecution is not something any of us want to face or believe is our calling, despite Jesus' words to the contrary in 2Timothy 3:12:

"Yea, and all that will live godly in Christ Jesus shall suffer persecution."

I think that most of us would far prefer God just burst into our lives with great revivals. However, a simple glance through history shows time and time again, that the power of Christianity has always shone in the midst of persecution and not through the presentation of the miraculous that tries to draw attention to God. Apart from some genuine moves of God that have produced a temporary revival, nearly all the really substantial and genuine 'new life' growth that has ever taken place throughout church history has been in times of serious persecution which those of us in the West have not really experienced for a long time. Certainly not the kind of persecution that is being experienced across so many other countries where Christians are being removed from their lands and tortured and killed, including parts of the Middle East and China.

There are literally thousands of martyrs in our time and hardly any real media coverage in the West, but there is plenty of news coverage about the plight of Muslims. The persecution that we in the West experience is subtler. Christians who stand up for the right to speak about their faith and declare the truth of the Bible are now being reprimanded and even prosecuted for so doing. But the times in which we now live, indicate that more serious persecution is coming and we need to ask ourselves - are we prepared? It is clear that the church in the West is now facing the most difficult time with the laws changing to make declaring the gospel and the truth of the Bible liable to offence and leading to possible prosecution for breaking hate laws.

Church that may have to go Underground

I believe that we are witnessing a new age of Christianity emerging that, whilst being true to scriptures and honouring

226

God, will bring a completely different understanding about how we 'do' church. It is what all those churches in China, Russia and elsewhere have had to learn about what it means to operate 'underground' in the face of severe persecution. It is where Christians form close knit spiritual bonds and relationships that enable them to stand together in the midst of such persecution and even to die for one another. This is what we see in the church throughout the New Testament, and Jesus told us clearly that anyone who chooses to follow him *will* be persecuted.

We must surely realise that we in the West have not understood what it means to suffer persecution for the sake of His name, certainly not for about 500 years or so. However, we are nearing a time, when we will understand, and then, for those who have grasped what church is meant to be and are filled with the Spirit, we will see the power of God come upon the church in ways unimaginable. No more will we be gathering in stadiums to listen to the great well-known leaders who come to lead us into the so-called signs and wonders and miracles ministries. No longer will we gather to ask the Holy Spirit to indwell our gatherings so we can get lost in a sense of worship, only to come out the same as we went in!

In Stan Firth's book, *Custom and Command*, he describes what he calls the 'Unstructured Church'. He wrote this book in 1996 and explained what he believed God showed him in the Scriptures. He gives us an idea about the sort of church that would be required as we approach the end of the end times. In 2010, fourteen years later, he wrote another book called *God's Remarkable Replacement Army*, based on a prophetic word that he had received from the Lord. In both these books he was convinced that the church structures that had previously existed for centuries would fall and need to be replaced by other 'unstructured' methods of 'doing church' together. I would recommend that people who wish to know more get hold of a copy of these books. I believe he is another example of the hundreds, if not thousands, of people throughout the world that God is speaking to along the same lines. Another really important best-selling book that was also written over twenty years ago, was *Houses that Change the World* by Wolfgang Simson, which also describes much about 'unstructured church'.

Having met Wolfgang a couple of times, as well as other church pioneers over the past 30 years and discussed their observations, I have found myself being challenged many times about the concept of 'church in the home'. I have also had various different church experiences which have led me to the conclusion that church in these last days will have to be quite different from that most of us in the West experience today. I have no doubt that many people will be called by The Lord to take a lead in it and others will follow. As with all new things, it first takes pioneers to lead. One way or another, I believe that the church of the future will return to the home and other private gatherings.

Church with Sound Biblical Oversight

I believe that in these last days, only those churches that are prepared to provide sound Biblical doctrine in respect of oversight in leadership as laid out in the scriptures of the New Testament will be able to take a stand and operate with power of the Holy Spirit. However, it seems that most evangelical churches have, these days, given way to the pressure of the world to conform to ideas of oversight that does not conform to Biblical doctrine. The Biblical command for male headship and oversight is no longer believed to be necessary. If we continue to apply the principles of exegesis to the interpretation of scripture and do not insist on our own understanding be applied (eisegesis) then it is very clear how the church should be governed and by whom. I realise that this is a controversial statement, but I do not believe that a church can declare it itself to be a place of sound in doctrine if it does not accept the Biblical call for male headship and male governance in the church. As the darkness grows darker in the days to come, and issues relating to male and female sexuality become more and more confused, it will only be those churches that remain obedient to the scriptures, as opposed to conforming to the world's values who will be able to stand.

Church that Prepares Leaders and Devoted Disciples of Jesus

In the book Matthew 28: 18-20, Jesus left his disciples with the following command:

Converging Signs and Rejection of Truth

Then Jesus came to them and said, "All authority in heaven and on earth has been given to me. Therefore go and make disciples of all nations, baptizing them in the name of the Father and of the Son and of the Holy Spirit, and teaching them to obey everything I have commanded you. And surely I am with you always, to the very end of the age."

We know therefore, that Jesus saw the church's most important priority in the days that lie ahead was to produce fully devoted followers of himself. Preparation and development of its leaders will be vital, with everything subordinated to this vitally important task. The clear purpose should be to teach fully devoted, spirit-filled, doctrinally sound believers to be completely submitted to Christ. To do this, however, would probably require a complete reappraisal of existing leadership teams in most churches and especially those responsible for teaching the Word of God.

What do we mean by 'fully devoted'? How can the level of devotion be measured and by whom? What might the consequences be for not being fully devoted? How do Elders ensure that they and their leaders remain fully devoted themselves? How do they ensure that they are fully accountable to their members and to each other? How much time is required by Elders to help grow leaders? The list goes on and on, but in my own church life, I have only once experienced a church that has worked to honour Christ in this way. My hope and prayer, is that this might be a wake-up call to leaders to consider the fact that, without strong leadership at all levels, it is unlikely that any church will automatically be able to stand firm in the light of the persecution that is coming.

No matter how we choose to look at the Western Church, it seems that the idea of developing fully devoted followers of Jesus Christ into His disciples, who are spiritually prepared to minister deeply into others the life changing Gospel, is dwindling. Sadly, such 'ministry' so often shows no sign of the Holy Spirit's power to change lives or bring the release that God would seek through the continued application of the Word of God. How many leaders challenge those under their care when they fall into sin with appropriate scripture? How many follow up those under their care, to hold them accountable for their subsequent actions? Without such dedication towards discipling others, there is every chance Christians will continue to sin and fail to move into the purposes of God.

The signs or events that are taking place worldwide, already outlined, can only be described as a series of tsunamis that are bearing down on the world and on the church. Those who have ever witnessed a real tsunami will recall what happens just before the real strength and power of the water hits. Before doing so, it is preceded with a time of peace and quiet as the tide seems to slowly drain the water away leaving a beautiful extended beach area with many people still playing and enjoying themselves. Then – suddenly - a roaring can be heard in the distance and one can see a huge head of water appear on the horizon as the sea gathers momentum and strength before returning with a ferocity that quickly overpowers all those still frolicking on the beach and goes on to destroy everything in sight. We saw a perfect example of this in 2012 when over 200,000 people were killed in the tsunami that followed a huge Indonesian earthquake. This is how I see much of the church in these days.

How are we to think about such things? Well, clearly there is an urgent need to prepare Christians to become strong and mature disciples of Jesus, as the Bible challenges us to do. The sweeping changes and disintegration of life as we now experience it can only be countered by knowing the Word of God and moving in the power of the Holy Spirit. It can only happen if we know Jesus as our friend and Saviour deep within and have learned, often through adversity, to trust Him implicitly. Any other form of 'nominal' Christianity will have no power to sustain let alone save. The big question is, how do we make such disciples in an age where life is relatively comfortable and where so many Christians' lives generally fail to look any different from any other? I believe that it will require nothing less than the complete re-prioritisation of time and energy away from 'worldly' things to focus on God's word. How many of us are prepared to do so?

Church Propelled or Discipleship Propelled?

One of the main questions that should cause all of us to really think about the way we 'do' church is: are Christians church propelled or discipleship propelled, because so many appear to be the former as they often become very engaged in 'channels of service' but without any real signs of being spirit-filled disciples in love with Jesus.

What happens when hostile governments come down heavily on Christianity? One, now retired, Christian pastor suggests that Christians may so easily turn out like pieces of wood carried along by the current of the church stream rather than becoming healthy fish with the inner motivation to swim in the right direction. Very challenging to be sure. I do not, however, believe that all arranged channels of service are of no use. Clearly, some are. Not only that, I am quite sure that there are many people in the community who see the light of Christ in those who come to serve them and that this may lead to people becoming Christians.

People, not Projects

Perhaps one of the more challenging comments some writers make about their understanding of church is: that it needs to be more about people than projects. It is clear that in many churches, projects are set up by leaders, not only to serve the community but to help provide opportunities for Christians to connect and hopefully witness to the community. I believe that such projects will need to be reviewed in the light of Jesus' mission statement and the clear Biblical command to spend time 'One Anothering'. So many Christians just submit to church structures in the desire to be obedient in their church service. Many simply like the social context but only a few take the opportunity to give people the gospel and I suggest that only a small number probably have any meaningful spiritual connection, with most relationships probably remaining on a surface level only, thus avoiding any real degree of truth or openness that can change lives.

One Anothering

Perhaps one the most profound observations about church came from our time spent in leading Alpha groups, which we did for many years. It was here that we saw people from all kinds of backgrounds come together and form closer relationships over a period of weeks. As they began to discover who Jesus was, why he died and what it meant for them personally, they opened up their lives to each other and often became the best of friends, which was more than surface deep. It meant people being prepared to minister to one another in the power of the Spirit and really caring for one another in all sorts of practical and spiritual ways. But these groups of people need to be small in number; say 8-10 at the most to enable them to truly 'know' each other and support each other through the good times and the bad. When persecution comes, they can be relied on not 'give one another up' The Bible has much to say about the idea of 'One Anothering'.

Is Church Service the same as Discipleship?

Converging Signs and Rejection of Truth

During my years in church life, my main areas of service have principally been involved with evangelism and discipleship. In the early years, I was always delighted and encouraged to see people come to faith and this became the main thrust of the ministry God called me to. In later years, when I saw new Christians struggling, I became more concerned about their integration with church life. I can remember several older Christians saying to me that they would recommend new Christians try to keep away from the church for as long as possible. Initially this puzzled me but, as the years went by and I saw what can happen in church life, I began to understand why they had said this. However, it remained a total contradiction to what Jesus expected and desired. This is one of the main reasons I have observed over the years why so many evangelists somehow restrict themselves solely to the work of evangelism. In this way they do not need to become involved with the work of integration of new Christians into local church fellowships; this is left up to church leaders.

In my later years, especially whilst in positions of leadership, discipleship became my main concern, but it has, all too often, seemed to me that discipleship in many churches in the Western world remains extremely weak. What do I mean by weak? Basically, that most church ministers and their leaders are either inadequately trained or even too busy to draw alongside and bring the Word of God to those under their care who are falling away under the influence of Iniquity. This means being prepared to confront sin in their love for their congregation. Is it easy to do? No, it is not, because it will not always be welcome. When confronted with the truth, there is always a choice. Do I hear what God is saying through His Word or do I block this revelation to my life and choose my own pathway? Only those churches with Christians filled with the Holy Spirit, who interact with each other on a regular basis, whilst speaking the truth in love, will enable people to become fully devoted followers of Christ.

What particularly strikes me, is the thought that multitudes of Christians may sadly not even survive if they found themselves outside the structures of the institutional church, especially in the midst of severe persecution. When I use the word institutional, I don't just mean traditional mainstream churches like the Anglican, Methodist or Baptist denominations, I also include many church streams that believe in Biblical leadership and discipleship. All too often people are not faced with the truth of scripture that will bring people to repentance, freedom in Christ and power in the Kingdom thereafter.

Church of Small Close Fellowship Networks

If churches operate in homes in underground movements, they will need to work out how they also move together within smaller networks. Clearly in times of heavy persecution this will require strategy similar to the underground movements that operated in countries like France, during the war. All effective churches need the four-fold ministries to include apostles, prophets, evangelists and pastor-teachers. (Ephesians 4). Obviously, these would need to be 'roving' ministries so to speak with those gifted by God to build up the body of Christ, teaching them to live as children of light, but without formal structure of a single church.

This is, after all, how churches have developed in countries like China and Russia as well as others. When Jesus said in the scriptures that a time is coming when the love of most will grow cold, and people will hand each other over to the authorities, it should be clear that we will only be able to form relationships with those who are experiencing the same presence of Christ as we are. It is only when you come into contact with others who understand the times, that you experience a strong sense of God's Holy Spirit. Somehow, He meets with you deeply and you just know you are in the presence other fellow believers who have an intimate relationship with Christ and with whom you could stand in these end times.

It is in the book of Acts that we see the first churches established and the fellowship that developed. We see the gospel being preached and the 'one anothering' that took place between the people as they listened to the word being taught and as they became obedient to the Apostles' teaching from the scriptures. The result as in Chapter 2: verse 47:

"praising God and having favour with all the people. And the Lord added to the church daily such as should be saved."

These were primarily Jews who had come to know their Messiah and they met in all kinds of places and particularly in homes. The churches were full of expectation. If you have ever been involved with leading a group of people from a state of unbelief to the knowledge and acceptance of Jesus as their Saviour, you will have seen a great miracle take place before your eyes. It changes your entire perception of how God can work amongst us. It is thoroughly exhilarating and life changing to see God at work. But the biggest challenge thereafter is to know how to introduce these brand-new Christians, into 'church'. I can recall so often, after the end of an evening together, when people had made their commitments to Christ, how they valued their new-found friendships and how they wanted to stay together. We often heard them say that they had seen what 'church' meant. However, once they were introduced to the established structure of church and attended with any degree of regularity, they so often began to question what they saw as a form of watered down Christianity that lacked the reality and openness they had experienced between each other. As a result, their enthusiasm was often dampened, as relationships so often just seemed to settle into nothing more than a nice social group that came together once a week to chat about the bible. Then, once they became involved with routine and church projects, the initial spark often seemed to lose its glow. Now, I know that many Christians would say that this always happens to new Christians. They say that we all go through a kind of honeymoon period. I agree to some extent but disagree that this lacklustre life as a Christian should be our continued experience thereafter.

I now believe that those who are 'born again' and desire to become disciples of Jesus can be identified by their hearts desire to hunger and thirst after righteousness through their desire to know the Word of God. In other words, to learn sound doctrine. The problem is that over these past 30-40 years, real close discipleship has not been seen with the same degree of importance as becoming a part of the routine of church programmes and projects. I do believe that most churches would say that they want to disciple people, but in the main, the commitment is lacking and doesn't even begin to resemble the type of discipleship that we see in the New Testament. Everything about church life so quickly becomes routine and project led rather than discipleship led. The freedom of the Holy Spirit is so often lost and it is not surprising how many people drift away from church or spend their lives searching for this experience that they once encountered. Despite all this, building God's Kingdom through his people remains the driving force behind all that we have been involved with since becoming Christians. But, the big question still remains, 'What Type of Church' is it that Jesus has in mind for the days that lie ahead?

Church that teaches its Children the Word of God

I believe that only those churches that understand the need to impress upon their children the importance of the Word of God will stand firm. It seems that so often these days, the young can so easily become victims of certain styles of evangelism, worship or leadership that has come from participation in church activities which then becomes the thermometer for commitment to Christ. In my own experience over the years, the most informative and constructive times of discipleship have been on a one-to-one basis. The most effective has been from what I would call 'loose' experiences, where meetings have been arranged, so to speak, by the Holy Spirit, where it becomes possible to simply chat through everyday life and to teach from the word of God directly into lives and see positive change. Unfortunately, so many parents today take no personal responsibility for so doing; they merely leave their church youth leaders or church leaders with this task.

In Deuteronomy 6:6-7 the Bible speaks about impressing on your children the word of God. In the New Testament and Colossians 3:16 it says, let the word dwell in you richly as you teach and admonish. The teaching that most Christians generally receive in churches today comes from a lecture style and not often through a conversational style which can engage people so much more with the truth of scripture. What should be evident from good teaching is good works – i.e. the fruits of the spirit. As we enter into the times to come, the main concern is that if people, and especially the young, are merely swept along by 'everything that is wonderful', then an active spirit-led Christian life based on sound doctrine isn't likely to emerge.

Church with Eyes to See and Ears to Hear

As I have stated throughout this book, my main aim is to bring an awareness to church members and church leaders about the times we are now in. It is a call for all those with eyes to see and ears to hear to look around and see what the world and the church is facing. I have always believed in the church and been involved in various forms of leadership during my church journey. I realise, only too well, the need to approach the subject of church with as much humility as possible. Leading churches is not an easy calling. However, the big question I am asking is, are we 'doing church' the way that I believe Jesus intended and if not, what are we going to do about it? I am very aware of the many leaders who have given their lives to building the church and that doing so is not a piece of cake. So, this book is not about bringing criticism about the church or about leaders. It is merely an attempt to discover what God is saying about His desires for church in the days to come.

Converging Signs and Rejection of Truth

What is the Spirit saying to your Church Today?

The question we must address in these times is, who are the people trying to bring warnings to the church and to the country in our day and how are we responding to them? Fortunately, there are a few leaders and church members of various denominations who do 'see' what is taking place in the world and where this is all heading in accordance with the scriptures. Some are endeavouring to bring warnings about how to prepare Gods people, but unfortunately the majority of Christians, who have lived in the comforts of our illusionary world for the past 70 years, remain locked into their understanding about how you live the Christian life and how you 'do' church.

Somehow, no matter what we might think or believe, people fail to understand just how powerful and important money has become in everyone's minds. Very few realise how it controls every single thing that we do or just how much it's power corrupts, even the most supposedly incorruptible. In the book 1 Timothy chapter 6, Paul speaks about the power of money to corrupt. However, it is indeed most interesting to note that before doing so, he speaks about people who become involved with false doctrine and those with godly teaching. He then moves on to those who become involved with unhealthy controversies that so often result in envy, strife, malicious talk, evil suspicions and constant friction. Interestingly he says that such things take place between men of corrupt minds who think that godliness is a means to financial gain. He then reminds us that we all came into the world with nothing and we will all leave the world with nothing;

therefore, we should be content in all circumstances whether we are rich or poor. Then, Paul makes a really important statement. In verse 10 he says:

"For the love of money is the root of all evil: which while some coveted after, they have erred from the faith, and pierced themselves through with many sorrows.'

Paul makes his big point. Unless we receive good teaching based on sound doctrine we are likely to go seriously astray. The love of Money is THE root of ALL evil. We might say that we don't love money. We might say that it is all God's money. We might say that money doesn't rule our lives. We might say all sorts of things but the question is, what would we do if we lost it all tomorrow? What would we do, if money disappeared from our various bank accounts or building societies or pension fund statements. What might we do then? Would we find our faith as strong in God, or would we become seriously depressed and lost because all our security had gone? The problem is that none of us dwells on such things because we don't really believe that this would happen. Why do we think that? What are our assumptions based on? What makes us think that everything we know about the monetary system is OK? Do any of us really understand what money actually is anyway? The answer is no. None of us really knows. In the chapter on of Money and Economics, I provided some understanding but, even now, I wonder if most readers have forgotten or do not think they really need to know or understand. You may have found it interesting for a moment, but, have since let these thoughts disappear from your mind.

The reason I have said all this, is because the reality is that our whole world's monetary system has been seriously weakened by the 2008 Global Debt Crisis and has now become even more liable to complete collapse than before, mostly the result of debt increasing since then. There is a mountain of evidence in the news every day that will show how delicate the system is and how easily it could be tipped into financial chaos. This time, however, the chaos would lead to severe social disruption, because if people suddenly woke up one day to find everything that they thought they owned on paper was relatively worthless they could easily elapse into severe depression and even Christians would find themselves having to reassess whether the faith that they thought they had in God was real at all.

We must all wake up to the fact that we are headed towards what many would call a financial Armageddon. It is not a question of whether the system will collapse but when. But we also need to realise that this is in line with Biblical prophecy and to expect it. We must all wake up to the fact that this country is no longer Christian and our governments are no longer prepared to support Christianity. Everything we understand about speaking out the gospel in our society is going to change. If church congregations find themselves in serious financial difficulties or unfair persecution how will this affect your church. How will it affect your teaching and how well will you be able to encourage people that it is all in accordance with prophecy? How many leaders will know their Bibles sufficiently well to be able to explain what the prophetic scriptures teach? How many leaders will you be able to rely on to take the strain and to encourage their group members to remain strong. How will the weak and vulnerable be able to function and who will support them? What will happen when the government takes away church charity rights that allow huge tax rebates? With reduced personal incomes, and reduced church income, how will the church survive with its current financial outlays or be able to repay huge loans? What will happen if church buildings cannot continue to operate as centres that proclaim the gospel when it is claimed to be hate speech? Where will church members meet if their buildings are no longer available for such use? How will church leaders be remunerated? How will church pastors be able to find the time to visit numerous members who become seriously depressed as a result of losing their jobs? What will happen when your own church members begin to lose their jobs through proclaiming the gospel or through artificial intelligence or robotics? The list of questions is endless but how many church leaders are even thinking about such things?

The daily propaganda in our mainstream news continues to send out false signals that all is well and we can look forward to a prosperous future. People continue to hear that an economy must be doing well when the prices of the stock markets and property prices are sky high, but these are the two main mechanisms used to blind the masses. The fact that all markets are now manipulated through the use of highly dangerous financial computerised algorithms give the appearance of being healthy, is keeping the people in the dark, just as happened so often before. The power of those controlling the debt-ridden world still seems to be intact for the time being.

As you study history, nothing changes about the insidiousness of power. Power always corrupts and absolute power always corrupts absolutely. Greed and power are the causes of massive accumulated wealth amongst the few super rich. As has been said so many times before, when people fail to learn from history, history is bound to repeat itself. If only history as a subject could have been taught over the past years by more imaginative and influential teachers, maybe this wouldn't be so. It is the same with the subject of money. If only people had been taught from their early years what money is and the difference between money and wealth. Without such knowledge about the 'Monetary System', people simply didn't know what to expect when the 2008 crisis occurred. They just became embroiled in a huge financial calamity that shocked everyone and they could not understand what was happening to them, their families or their financial security.

This is what happened with the 'Monetary System' in Germany when outrageous levels of inflation suddenly destroyed the German D-Mark. It is what happened in 1929 when the stock-market crashed, leaving the world with a massive depression for years. It is as a result of this seemingly, purposeful lack of education, that people are going to be fooled and deceived when it comes to the anti-Christ gaining power over the monetary system of the world.

Let me end this chapter by reiterating that this is not about trying to suggest that everything that goes on in the name of church is wrong. What I am saying is that I believe that in the days that lie ahead, church is going to have to be transformed into something that is fit for purpose. I believe that Jesus knows everything that has been achieved to date throughout all history by all those dedicated pastors, teachers, evangelists and prophets. But, He is now going to have to move into a different gear, so to speak. The true church of the end times will be strong and effective because Jesus will make it so, but there is going to have to be a great deal of sifting. All we have to decide is, what do we believe Jesus is saying to those of us today who have any responsibility in helping to build His church? Are we keeping watch? Are we making disciples ready for Jesus return? Are we bringing the Word of God to those falling into sin? Have we done what Jesus is asking in these days? Let us seek God's grace in this vitally important task that lies ahead and may the Lord who knows everything from beginning to end bless you and your families.

Chapter 12: What does the Future have in Store?

There is real fascination with the future and what it might have in store for us. That is why so many people read their horoscopes in the newspapers each day and why they seek out those who claim to be able to make accurate predictions. But the truth is that most predictions are notoriously inaccurate. The success rate is very minimal compared with one other source that has, over thousands of years, proven to be accurate 100 percent of the time - the Bible. In the Bible, God reveals his purposes for mankind. Purposes that would be fulfilled in the person of Jesus Christ through both his First and Second Comings. If we want to know the future, then we need to seek the God of the Bible.

As I have already explained in previous chapters, it is because of the rise of deception that the truth of the Bible is being questioned. Many ask whether it is still acceptable in our post-modern, relativist, Western society where there is no such thing as absolute truth. The deception, Satanic in nature, is causing heavier opposition to the preaching of God's word and persecution of Christians is increasing day by day, more than has been known for hundreds of years. Confusion, doubt and fear is increasing and this is seriously concerning, because the world is moving very much closer to the return of Jesus and there is virtually no teaching in local churches about what will happen or how Christians should be prepared.

The passion of Jesus Christ stands alone as the most important event ever known. The Bible tells us that long before the world began, God had planned that the crucifixion of Jesus would be the means by which Iniquity (sin) would be dealt with. That it would be the only payment that could reconcile sinners, i.e. those born into iniquity, back to a relationship with a holy and loving God. In 1 Peter 1:19-20 it says:

"But with the precious blood of Christ, as of a lamb without blemish and without spot: Who verily was foreordained before the foundation of the world, but was manifest in these last times for you."

Throughout the Bible, God has provided the human race with a roadmap for life. Through his prophets, he revealed his purposes for mankind well ahead of time, so they might prepare for what lay ahead. These prophets spoke of things that mankind should watch for so that the Messiah would be recognized and believed. These signs or prophecies in the Old Testament were completed in 450 B.C and thus written hundreds of years before Jesus' birth. They contain over 300 prophecies that Jesus fulfilled through His life, death and resurrection. Mathematically speaking, the odds of anyone fulfilling this amount of prophecy are simply staggering. Mathematicians put it this way:

1 person fulfilling 8 prophecies: 1 in 100,000,000,000,000,000. 1 person fulfilling 48 prophecies: 1 chance in 10 to the 157th power. 1 person fulfilling 300+ prophecies: Only Jesus!

It is the magnificent detail of these prophecies that marks the Bible as the inspired Word of God. Only God could foreknow and accomplish all that was written about the Christ. The historical accuracy and reliability sets the Bible apart from any other book or record. The Bible is superior to any other ancient writings and God gave us these prophecies to build our faith and point the way to His Son.

Where are You Placing Your Hope?

When we think about the world in which we live and the future that awaits us, we easily forget how we are inadvertently influenced by so many sources. In the Western World, we are literally bombarded with images every day that become imprinted in our minds, consciously or unconsciously. Television and cinema programmes, together with the required sprinkling of advertisements, are there to titillate our desires. Billboards and poster advertisements seek our attention during the boredom of train and bus journeys to work. Large moving pictures framed in strategically placed positions grab our attention as we walk through shopping centres. They are all attempting to appeal to our innermost wants, needs and desires, and very often do so by entering our subconscious minds. There they fester until some part of our desire mechanism is triggered by the image that causes us to want something, whether we need it or not. This is the technological, materialistic and consumer driven world in which we live.

Living in such a technological age, we are also bombarded with images of what life could be. When we read novels or watch movies about the future, we each get an idea of what is possible according to the author or the filmmaker. Sometimes we are thrust into a world that is filled with even more pain than we experience on earth and sometimes we can be transported to a world of beauty, peace and tranquillity. Because of man's abilities to create images of how things could be, the possibilities seem endless. But these are just dreams about what the future might hold, they are not the reality.

But God does reveal what is in store for the human race and particularly about what will happen as we enter into the last days. Throughout the pages of the Bible, both in the Old Testament and in the New Testament, God gave specific visions to his servants the prophets but none more so than the last of his Apostles, John. In Revelation 1:19, He put it this way:

"Write the things which thou hast seen, and the things which are, and the things which shall be hereafter."

This scripture speaks about the things which John has already seen, things that he is experiencing in the now and things that shall be experienced in the future. How amazing for John. It was like God was penetrating his mind and senses with 3D images that he had never seen before. God then asked John to write down the things that He was showing him and he had to use the limitations of his own language to try and reveal the pictures and the images he was seeing in words, two thousand years before they were to come into being. Seems like a pretty tall order! But John did it through the illumination of the Holy Spirit and it has been recorded for mankind to read and receive ever since. But God has said that we are to read it and listen to it out loud. More importantly, we are to take what is being said *to heart*! That is how we will be blessed. It is a heart thing, not an intellectual thing just for scholars to argue about as they so often do. Jesus told us in his opening words in the book of Revelation that anyone who hears and received these words and **who keeps them** will be blessed.

"The Revelation of Jesus Christ, which God gave unto him, to shew unto his servants things which must shortly come to pass; and he sent and signified it by his angel unto his servant John: Who bare record of the word of

*God, and of the testimony of Jesus Christ, and of all things that he saw. Blessed is he that readeth, and they that hear the words of this prophecy, and keep **(tereo)** those things which are written therein: for the time is at hand."* (Revelation 1:1-3)

The word **'Keep'** in the Greek is *"tereo"* and it means: To watch, to guard properly by keeping an eye on for personal ends, to hold fast, to serve. All those clever theologians who think that they can simply study the text in their own wisdom are seriously missing the point. These words are received by *revelation* from the spirit of God, that is, IF the spirit of God lives in you:

"But if the Spirit of him that raised up Jesus from the dead dwell in you, he that raised up Christ from the dead shall also quicken your mortal bodies by his Spirit that dwelleth in you." (Romans 8:11)

We are to treasure these words in our hearts and meditate on them to receive the blessings God has in store. But this will depend upon whether you are reconciled with God in the first place; otherwise they are just words. The text is of little use if only used by scholars and intellectuals for knowledge's sake.

A Magnificent Vision of the Future

The Bible says, in the Gospel of John, chapter 3, that God so loved the world that he gave (sacrificed) his only Son Jesus Christ, so that everyone who believes in his heart and confesses with his mouth that Jesus is Lord and God, will be saved. This is a revelation from God, who draws those who are being saved to himself, through Jesus Christ. No-one can find God until this reality strikes at the heart of our human soul and we see the truth that sets men free. Jesus said that there is no other way to God the Father other than through himself. Once this truth becomes a revelation that moves from our heads to our hearts, we become, as the Bible says, 'born again' by the Holy Spirit of God and followers of Christ. As we submit to the work of Holy Spirit, whose job is to transform us into the likeness of Christ during our daily lives, we can look forward to a magnificent future that is beyond the human capacity to describe. We need have no fear about the future even though, from a worldly point of view, things can look pretty grim. But it is in the book of Revelation we read Jesus' last words to humanity about the hope we have for the future.

The question is, why did God speak to John this way? What was God thinking of? How could God expect a mere man, who lived in a certain culture, during a particular moment in history, to grasp what God was trying to show him about the future? Somehow John was able to transcribe into words some of the magnificent vision of the future. God wanted readers throughout history to understand how the events of the future would unfold in order to bring not just a sense of reality but above all hope. These revelations from God must have been so hard for John to describe in words. God was showing him events and images about which he would have had no understanding at all. Images and symbols that would depict events that would be happening in the future. But God is God. God has done the most amazing things, as we are told in numerous stories throughout the Bible. The most amazing is when He sent His son to live with us on earth as a man for three full years, during which short period of time, he would change the entire world forever. In the Bible God has shown us how to live in harmony with each other and what love is. But God has also shown us what iniquity is and what mankind can be like, as well as the things he is capable of, if left to his own devices. He has shown us the extent of evil that man can become involved with and the destruction that he can bring upon himself and others.

God is revealing all this to John because he wants to make us aware that although our journey has been through a rough desert, so to speak, subjected to all the ups and downs of this life in a world where sin is rampant and which will progressively get worse, there is a hope beyond anything we could imagine. He is saying that he has a destiny beyond our wildest dreams for those who love him. The Bible reveals the answers to the future through the prophetic scriptures written thousands of years ago and none more so than in the books of the Prophets and in particular Daniel, Zechariah, Matthew, Mark and Luke, the books of 1 and 2 Thessalonians and the book of Revelation. They provide the answers to what lies ahead. I have already outlined some of the detail in previous chapters.

Converging Signs and Rejection of Truth

Now, God reveals to John what will happen as he begins to bring his judgments on a world that refuses to accept the truth about his Son, Jesus Christ. He reveals the extent of his wrath in ways that most people will find hard to believe about a loving God. But as these judgements progress, we see the same reaction from people that we saw in the book of Exodus, when, after having set the Israelites free from years of slavery, the Pharaoh of Egypt decided to hunt them down again until they seemed to be trapped at the edge of the Red Sea. Then, we read that God performed the most amazing miracle; the opening of the Red Sea which enabled the Israelites to cross to safety, whilst He held the Egyptian army back by a pillar of Fire out of the heavens. This must have been a truly spectacular to witness and we get to see a portrayal of it in the old 1950s film *'The Ten Commandments'* with Charlton Heston. However, later on, whilst in the desert, despite these outstanding miracles by God, we go on to read that the people began to curse him, because he had, in their eyes, led them to a place with no apparent hope. This is what happens in the last days, during God's last judgments on the earth. People literally curse God to his face as his judgment falls. I believe that this proves beyond doubt that Iniquity, i.e. the sin humanity is born with, is so strong that man can curse God even when they know it is God bringing judgement upon them. We should now understand why it took the cross of Christ to free mankind from the power of this iniquity that is killing each and every one of us physically and spiritually until we accept the truth of Christ in our lives. You can read of these progressive judgments in the book of Revelation.

At the conclusion of these terrible judgements, Jesus begins his thousand-year reign on the earth, known as the Millennium. Can any of us even understand how God will repair the earth that was shattered during the time of His wrath and prepare to rule with Christ during the next thousand years? No, but God clearly does so, and the Bible goes on to speak of his followers who have overcome the power of Satan, reigning with Christ and ruling cities. It seems too much for us all to take in.

This indicates a new beginning for mankind but this is still not yet the end of the story. God then reveals what will happen after the end of this millennial period when he will finally resurrect everyone who has ever lived, to stand before him in what is described as the Great White Throne Judgment. This will be when every person will be held accountable for every word that they had ever spoken and every action taken whilst on the earth. They will come before the final judgment seat of God.

Will you be an 'Overcomer'?

It is the destiny of man to live on this earth for a few years although he doesn't know how long. He has been given the opportunity to live according to God's commandments or to live independently from God. He has been given the power of choice. He can love or hate. He can choose God as his friend or not. He can deny that God even exists. However, at the end of his life he will know for sure whether there is life beyond the grave. We will all find out as we stand before a Holy God and become answerable only to Him. Jesus tells us:

"But I say unto you, that every idle word that men shall speak, they shall give account thereof in the day of judgment." (Matthew 12:36)

Until then, man can go on believing whatever he chooses. In the end, whether he chooses to believe what the Bible says or not, does not change the fact that he will stand before a righteous God, who will judge the way he lived his life. If he has rejected God throughout life by ignoring His Word, then God says he will automatically have chosen his pathway into the future. What a thought!

"I counsel thee to buy of me gold tried in the fire, that thou mayest be rich; and white raiment, that thou mayest be clothed, and that the shame of thy nakedness do not appear; and anoint thine eyes with eyesalve, that thou mayest see. As many as I love, I rebuke and chasten: be zealous therefore, and repent. Behold, I stand at the door, and knock: if any man hear my voice, and open the door, I will come in to him, and will sup with him, and he with me. To him that overcometh will I grant to sit with me in my throne, even as I also overcame, and am set down with my Father in his throne"

So, what does Jesus mean? In the book of Revelation, we see Jesus speaking to the churches in the first three chapters where he ends each section challenging each church in the same way - will they be those who overcome. Jesus says what will happen to all of us if we too ensure that we are overcomers:

they will eat from the tree of life (2:7); *be unharmed by the second death* (2:11); *eat from the hidden manna and be given a new name* (2:17); *have authority over the nations* (2:26) *be clothed with white garments* (3:5); *be made a permanent pillar in the house of God* (3:12); *and sit with Jesus on his throne* (3:21).

But Jesus told us that staying true to him would not be easy. He told us that if he was persecuted so would we. In fact, we would be hated because of his name (Mark13:13). He told us that he who stands firm to the end will be saved (Matthew 24:13)

Many believers in Christ will have been told that once they are saved and are true believers, they will become 'overcomers' automatically (1John 5:4). Whilst there is truth in this, because our salvation depends entirely on the work of Christ in his death on the cross, we also have a responsibility to work out our salvation with fear and trepidation (Philippians 2:12). We have moved positionally as it were, into the kingdom of light, but if all believers are overcomers automatically regardless of what they do here and now, saying in effect – I am saved and it doesn't matter whether I live a carnal life or not, then this must be held against the scripture in 1 Corinthians 3:13-18 that says:

Converging Signs and Rejection of Truth

"Every man's work shall be made manifest: for the day shall declare it, because it shall be revealed by fire; and the fire shall try every man's work of what sort it is. If any man's work abide which he hath built thereupon, he shall receive a reward. If any man's work shall be burned, he shall suffer loss: but he himself shall be saved; yet so as by fire. Know ye not that ye are the temple of God, and that the Spirit of God dwelleth in you? If any man defile the temple of God, him shall God destroy; for the temple of God is holy, which temple ye are. Let no man deceive himself. If any man among you seemeth to be wise in this world, let him become a fool, that he may be wise."

Most theologians agree that Jesus intended his words in the book of Revelation to be applicable throughout all of church history, but if we look at numerous prophetic scriptures that speak of the end times, we can see only too clearly that they apply to the church of these days more so than any time in history. To the church of Laodicea for example, Jesus warns that 'he is about to spit it out of his mouth'. He is telling us that if we think we are rich, to put salve on our eyes and repent in order to recognise that we are in fact *'wretched, pitiful, poor, blind and naked'*.

Dark or Light – Your Choice!

Dark clouds have been gathering for many years, but I believe that the final convergence of events is taking place across the globe. These events are not only taking place on an exponential basis but alongside Biblical signs, like those now taking place in Israel where we see not only the Jews returning to Israel but also the preparations for the building of the third temple and the reintroduction of the sacrificial practices. I believe these all indicate the growing nearness to the most significant events of all time as prophesied throughout the Bible. First, the arrival in the temple in Jerusalem of the feet of the one the Bible calls the anti-Christ who will reign for seven years. Next, the return of the feet of Jesus Christ touching down again in Jerusalem at his Second Coming in exactly the same place from which he ascended to the right hand of God after his resurrection. He promised his disciples that he would do this and those alive will see it happen.

As we draw to a conclusion in this final chapter and look through the illusion of our times, holding events up to scrutiny and comparing them with the numerous prophetic scriptures in the Bible, we will hopefully begin to form a very different viewpoint about what is actually unfolding before our very eyes and see more clearly into the future. It might enable us to change our outlook on life, unless we have settled into a comfortable Western Christian existence. We are promised by Jesus that if we open our eyes, *"The Truth will set us Free",* and that God will give us a sense of peace and security even in the midst of turmoil as we earnestly seek His guidance as to what our part to play might be during the times to come. The truth is, that the Western world has been exposed to unimaginable amounts of change over comparatively few years, which is now happening on an exponential basis. But Jesus himself said this would happen. He said events and signs would grow in number and intensity before his Second Coming. (Matthew 24:8)

Most people want reason for hope, not just for their own sake but for the sake of their children and their grandchildren, and they look for it in many different ways. Many still believe that the mess in the world can be turned around and that positive people with a positive attitude will give rise to hope. They often allow themselves to be persuaded by clever motivational speakers or even church leaders who preach that the Bible needs to be re-interpreted in line with our Western post-modern culture, in order to communicate with the millions of people who no longer find the traditional interpretation of the Word of God acceptable. Many people assume that we are merely going through another cycle of life and that we can overcome all obstacles with all our combined human ingenuity. Soon we will all come face to face with Jesus through whom the whole universe was made.

"For by him were all things created, that are in heaven, and that are in earth, visible and invisible, whether they be thrones, or dominions, or principalities, or powers: all things were created by him, and for him." (Colossians 1:16)

Our Final Decision

When it comes to the Christian faith, there are only two main groups into which people fall when considering the future: those who have faith in the redemption of Christ and those who don't. Agnostics claim to have no religious affiliation and, as a result, they don't know what they believe. Atheists claim to be sure about what they don't believe even though they have no proof. To be Christian means having accepted the truth about who Jesus was, why he came and why he had to die on the cross. Jesus said that this revelation will bring us to repentance which will be followed by a new birth experience. This will bring into focus the whole purpose of our being and our purpose here on earth. It will also bring a realisation of the truth of our 'being gathered together' (*harpazo*) with Him as we are led into the incredible future that God promises those who love Him. *This* was the dream that God gave us thirty years ago and that has given us the strength to go on working out our faith through thick and thin. It is here we see the truth of the scriptures revealed as Jesus receives all his own children, meeting them in the air as we can read in 1Thessalonians Chapter 4, verses 14-18:

*"For if we believe that Jesus died and rose again, even so them also which sleep in Jesus will God bring with him. For this we say unto you by the word of the Lord, that we which are alive and remain unto the coming of the Lord shall not **prevent** them which are asleep. For the Lord himself shall descend from heaven with a shout, with the voice of the archangel, and with the trump of God: and the dead in Christ shall rise first: Then we which are alive and remain shall be caught up together with them in the clouds, to meet the Lord in the air: and so shall we ever be with the Lord. Wherefore comfort one another with these words.*

Converging Signs and Rejection of Truth

The Greek word used in verse 15 for prevent is *"phthano"* which means anticipate or precede, i.e. to have arrived at already.

The final chapters of the book of Revelation show the incredible future that lies ahead for believers in Christ. What are you going to decide? It's your choice: Man's Rule or God's Rule? I believe that this message is from the Lord and I pray that all those with eyes to see and ears to hear will be able to respond, as we all prepare for the next and greatest revelation the world has ever seen or will see again - the return of Jesus Christ to rule on planet earth.

The intention of this book was to provide only an outline of what I observe, as it is my hope that people will be prompted to carry on with their own research into the detail and thus gain a 'worldly' and Biblical perspective for themselves. Perhaps most importantly, I believe that I have been given this opportunity to try to explain to a wider audience the reality of the times, but also the hope to which we have been called. No matter how dire things might appear, God can enter into a person's life quite unexpectedly and change everything for ever. He did it for me and he can do it for you. Once we allow Jesus in, we no longer need to despair, no matter how overwhelming and desperate things may appear. Instead, we can rest in the knowledge that He will be with us through all that is to come in the most miraculous of ways. As darkness grows darker, light will shine brighter. These last days will be the most productive that the world has ever known in terms of evangelism. All those born again, Spirit-filled Christians who have given their lives to Jesus will be in the forefront of this great battle. All born-again Christians will be 'snatched up' to meet Jesus in the clouds, with the dead in Christ first. This is why you hear Christians sometimes sing, "What a Saviour". May God bless you and your families as we move into the days that lie ahead, and don't forget to look up as the scriptures say:

"And when these things begin to come to pass, then look up, and lift up your heads; for your redemption draweth nigh." (Luke 21:28)

References and Resources

David Watson: Is Anyone There?
Tim Farron avoids saying whether he considers gay sex is a sin
https://www.theguardian.com/politics/2015/jul/18/tim-farron-avoids-saying-whether-he-sees-gay-sex-as-a-sin
Tim Farron as Liberal Democrat leader
https://www.theguardian.com/uk-news/blog/live/2017/jun/14/david-cameron-suggests-softer-brexit-as-may-weighs-options-politics-live?page=with:block-59417521e4b0240ef76147b0#block-59417521e4b0240ef76147b0
Trader Interview on BBC World News 28th September 2011 -
Goldman Sachs Rules the World
https://www.youtube.com/watch?v=eEV3zJbahvM&frags=pl%2Cwn
Angry Queen - https://www.express.co.uk/news/uk/69678/Angry-Queen-asks-Why-didn-t-anyone-see-the-credit-crunch-coming
05.11.2008
Time to stop this pretence – economics is not science by Liam
Halligan
https://www.telegraph.co.uk/finance/comment/10390981/Time-to-stop-this-pretence-economics-is-not-science.html
Don't let the Nobel prize fool you. Economics is not a science –
Joris Luyendijk
https://www.theguardian.com/commentisfree/2015/oct/11/nobel-prize-economics-not-science-hubris-disaster
Positive Money Web Site - The Proof that Banks Create Money
http://positivemoney.org/how-money-works/proof-that-banks-create-money/
**Bank of England - Money in the modern economy: an
introduction** By Michael McLeay, Amar Radia and Ryland Thomas
of the Bank's Monetary Analysis Directorate.
https://www.bankofengland.co.uk/-/media/boe/files/quarterly-bulletin/2014/money-in-the-modern-economy-an-introduction.pdf?la=en&hash=E43CDFDBB5A23D672F4D09B13D F135E6715EEDAC
Founder of the World Economic Forum
https://www.weforum.org/about/klaus-schwab

Converging Signs and Rejection of Truth

What price the new democracy? Goldman Sachs conquers Europe
https://www.independent.co.uk/news/business/analysis-and-features/what-price-the-new-democracy-goldman-sachs-conquers-europe-6264091.html
Simon Johnson – Former Chief Economist of the International Monetary Fund
https://en.wikipedia.org/wiki/Simon_Johnson_(economist)
David Cameron gets award for his role in introducing Gay Marriage – One of my greatest achievements
https://www.theguardian.com/politics/2016/oct/26/david-cameron-award-same-sex-marriage-pinknews - 26.10.2016
David Cameron - One of my proudest moments
https://www.pinknews.co.uk/privacy-policy/ - 28.05.2018
'95% of the earth's population are breathing dangerously high air pollution.
https://www.independent.co.uk/environment/air-pollution-quality-cities-health-effects-institute-environment-poverty-who-a8308856.html
https://www.theguardian.com/environment/2018/apr/17/more-than-95-of-worlds-population-breathe-dangerous-air-major-study-finds
David Pawson -Islam Challenge to Christians
Putin: The West has no morals
https://www.youtube.com/watch?v=q5pSe2zRaQI
Putin warns US 'you are in violation of EVERYTHING'
https://www.youtube.com/watch?v=7mBttPNP17k
Tony Blair denies praying with George Bush
https://www.theguardian.com/politics/2012/jul/25/tony-blair-denies-praying-george-bush
Blair 'prayed to God' over Iraq
http://news.bbc.co.uk/1/hi/4772142.stm
Unease as Blair lays soul bare
https://www.theguardian.com/politics/2003/may/04/uk.tonyblair
Foreign interventions by the United States
https://en.wikipedia.org/wiki/Foreign_interventions_by_the_United_States
Global Policy Forum

https://www.globalpolicy.org/us-westward-expansion/26024-us-interventions.html

Oxfam -1% Bagged 82% of world wealth in 2017
https://www.oxfam.org/en/pressroom/pressreleases/2018-01-22/richest-1-percent-bagged-82-percent-wealth-created-last-year

David Robertson: Blog (Weeflea.com)
https://theweeflea.com/?s=european+union

Bill Gates and Steve Jobs explain the Internet
https://www.youtube.com/watch?v=6F8oCDWcbSc

Panorama July 2018: Smart Phones: The Dark Side
https://www.bbc.co.uk/programmes/b0b9dzb6

Scientists Warn of Potential Health Effects Report 13ᵗʰ September 2017
https://drive.google.com/file/d/0B14R6QNkmaXuelFrNWRQcThNV0U/view

To the United Nations, World Health Organisation and United Nations Environment Programme: International Appeal: Scientists call for Protection from Non-ionizing Electromagnetic Field Exposure –
https://www.researchgate.net/publication/298533680 International Appeal Scientists call for protection from non-ionizing electromagnetic field exposure

Earth Now - https://techcrunch.com/2018/04/18/earthnow-promises-real-time-views-of-the-whole-planet-from-a-new-satellite-constellation/?guccounter=2

World-Wide Mass Animal Death Statistics on End-Times Prophecy web site http://www.end-times-prophecy.org/animal-deaths-birds-fish-end-times.html

C.S Lewis "Mere Christianity"

Council of Foreign Relations (CFR) is an independent, non-

partisan member organization, think tank, and publisher.
https://www.cfr.org/

Converging Signs and Rejection of Truth

Bilderberg Group - What actually happens at the world's most secret annual Conference of European and North American political elite
http://www.bilderbergmeetings.org/
Independent Newspaper 7th June 2016
https://www.independent.co.uk/news/world/bilderberg-group-meeting-what-is-it-and-who-is-attending-global-elites-a7069561.html
Bankers – Rothschild Group and Rockefeller's
https://www.worldfinance.com/markets/the-history-of-the-rockefeller-family
Rothschild: quote Control the Money
https://en.wikiquote.org/wiki/Conspiracy
The Nixon Shock
https://history.state.gov/milestones/1969-1976/nixon-shock
CIPS – China Interbank Payment System
SWIFT – Society for Worldwide Interbank Financial Telecommunication
United Nations 2030 Agenda - The Sustainable Development Goals (SDGs) - also known as the Global Goals for Sustainable Development - are a collection of 17 global goals set by the United Nations. ... The SDGs are also known as "Transforming our World:
Professor Stephen Hawking – "we can't go on ignoring inequality, because we have the means to destroy our world but not the means to escape it" – Guardian Newspaper 01.12.2016
https://www.theguardian.com/commentisfree/2016/dec/01/stephen-hawking-dangerous-time-planet-inequality
Geo-Engineering watch.com
John Perkins: Confessions of an Economic Hitman
Sam Solomon: Not the Same God (Islam)
Munich Security Conference is an annual conference on international security policy that has taken place in Munich, Bavaria since 1963
Melanie Phillips web site at http://www.melaniephillips.com.
Ann Pettifor: The Coming First World Debt Crisis'– Amazon
Ann Pettifor: The Production of Money: How to Break the Power of Bankers

Converging Signs and Rejection of Truth

David Cameron quote: 'We are all in it together' – Independent 29th January 2012
Positive Money says only 1 in 10 understand that Banks create Money – www.positivemoney.org
Confirmation from Bank of England that Banks create money - http://positivemoney.org/how-money-works/proof-that-banks-create-money/
Ray Kurzweil – https://futurism.com/kurzweil-claims-that-the-singularity-will-happen-by-2045/
Ray Kurzweil https://en.wikipedia.org/wiki/Ray_Kurzweil
Katherine Albrecht: Spychips https://www.amazon.com/Spychips-Major-Corporations-Government-Purchase/dp/0452287669
Fourth Industrial Revolution - https://www.weforum.org/agenda/2016/01/the-fourth-industrial-revolution-what-it-means-and-how-to-respond/
C.S. Lewis: The Screwtape Letters
Billy Graham preaching on the Christian Life and about Sin – numerous You Tube Videos
https://www.youtube.com/watch?v=1aZoqIwHsdM
https://www.youtube.com/watch?v=ei_eIL08vbs
Adolf Hitler: Mein Kampf (My Struggle) – Amazon
Bonhoeffer: Pastor, Martyr, Prophet, Spy: Eric Metaxas and Timothy J. Keller:
Stan Firth: Custom and Command – Amazon Books
Stan Firth: God's Remarkable Army
Wolfgang Simson: Houses that Change the World
The Coming Convergence' Film
https://www.amazon.co.uk/Coming-Convergence-Jack-Hibbs/dp/B06XSPZFCG/ref=sr_1_1?s=dvd&ie=UTF8&qid=152449 4681&sr=8-1&keywords=the+coming+convergence
James Jacob Prasch: Harpazo
James Jacob Prasch: Shadows of the Beast
James Jacob Prasch: The Dilemma of Laodicea
James Jacob Prasch: The Daniel Factor
Graham Bridger: The Great Last Days Money Deception

Converging Signs and Rejection of Truth

Graham Bridger The Global Debt Time Bomb
Harold Van B. Cleveland et al: Money and the Coming World Order
Todd Huizinga: The New Totalitarian Temptation: Global Governance and the Crisis of Democracy in Europe
David Platt Book: "Counter Culture"
Jonathon Van Maren: The Culture War
R. S. Harris: Is there a Case for Same Sex Marriage?
Dmitry Orlov: The Five Stages of Collapse
Tony Pearce: Countdown to Calamity
Steve Maltz: Into the Lion's Den

Printed in Great Britain
by Amazon